THE ROADS WE TRAVELED

Roberto —

You live in my life —

Parece que fue Ayer —

We need you to help our kids in schools — Press on my friend!

Dr. Carl
Tor Oma

THE ROADS WE TRAVELED

(Los Caminos Que Viajamos)

Dr. Tony Carvajal

Copyright © 2015 by Dr. Tony Carvajal.

ISBN: Softcover   978-1-5035-6435-0
         eBook   978-1-5035-6434-3

All rights reserved. No part of this book may be reproduced or transmitted in any form or by any means, electronic or mechanical, including photocopying, recording, or by any information storage and retrieval system, without permission in writing from the copyright owner.

Any people depicted in stock imagery provided by Thinkstock are models, and such images are being used for illustrative purposes only.
Certain stock imagery © Thinkstock.

Print information available on the last page.

Rev. date: 05/06/2015

To order additional copies of this book, contact:
Xlibris
1-888-795-4274
www.Xlibris.com
Orders@Xlibris.com

CONTENTS

Acknowledgements..xi
Foreword..xiii
Prologue...xv

PART ONE

The Way It Was

Chapter 1   A New World Indeed..3
Chapter 2   From River to Land They All Came to America 9
Chapter 3   Mañana de Carnaval (Morning of the Carnival)......... 15
Chapter 4   Tempest in a Teapot.. 19
Chapter 5   Pain and Healing Changes Everything 22
Chapter 6   The Sun Also Rises..25

PART TWO

The Way We Were

Chapter 7   Angelitos Negros (Little Black Angels).........................49
Chapter 8   In Search of a Better Life 56
Chapter 9   The Days the Rains Came 58
Chapter 10   Exodus to San José...61
Chapter 11   The Pot of Gold At Last 65
Chapter 12   It Was a Glowing and Fantastic Place 71
Chapter 13   Where Did All The Flowers Go..................................75
Chapter 14   A Difficult Transition 79
Chapter 15   A Dual Personality...83
Chapter 16   Miracle of Miracles..90

Chapter 17 Precious Slices of Life 92
Chapter 18 Superman Drops His Cape 97
Chapter 19 A Three Ring Circus 102
Chapter 20 I Know You Found a Happy Home 106
Chapter 21 I Walked Alone 109
Chapter 22 An 'aha' Moment 114
Chapter 23 I Welcomed My New World 115
Chapter 24 An Unwelcomed Message from America 119
Chapter 25 Time to Call It a Day 122
Chapter 26 Scholarship 128
Chapter 27 There Simply Was Not a More Congenial Spot 133
Chapter 28 Pocket Change Galore 136
Chapter 29 Un Mundo Raro (A Rare World) 139
Chapter 30 In Search of New Paths 142
Chapter 31 Barnum and Bailey Would be Appalled 148
Chapter 32 Begin the Beguine "Volver a Empezar" 150
Chapter 33 A New Reality 153

PART THREE

Where We Are Today

PART FOUR

Significant Truths and Revelations

Chapter 34 Essential Memories (Recuerdos Esenciales) 223
Chapter 35 Conclusion 231

Epilogue 239
Bibliography 243
End notes 245

For my loving sister, Magdalena Carvajal,
a woman of courage

"Though nothing can bring back the hour
of splendor in the grass, of glory in the flower,
we will grieve not, rather find strength in what remains behind…
Thanks to the human heart by which we live.
Thanks to its tenderness, its joys, and fears."

William Wordsworth

"Living on the margin either bums you out and kills you, or it turns you into a dreamer….if these dreamers are liberated, if they are brought back into the arms of society, they become the architects of the new community."

Judith Snow

ACKNOWLEDGEMENTS

The abundant love and support that inspired the writing of this book was enormous. I am thankful for the words of encouragement that I received from my wife Joanie, my daughters; Carmela and Jennifer, and my son, Marc Anthony.

My daughter, Carmela Carvajal Kim, provided her artistic editorial skills and talents as she scrutinized each major part of the book with a sensitive and personal flare. I am indebted to her for her staunch and professional advice.

Additionally, my sisters, Amparo Rosen and Magdalena Carvajal, were consistently willing, aptly able to monitor, and advise me on the significant aspects of family developments as each phase was completed. Both of them contributed clarity of substance when specific passages of our family history were vague and unclear.

The admirable contributions of lifelong relatives and friends who had been my classmates throughout my life, were of central importance to this memoir. Their conscientious responses, both written and oral, defined the caring and personal nature of the narrative. Without these significant relationships, this book would not have evolved in the manner that it did.

I was immensely fortunate to have a cadre of caring individuals who inspired me to write this book. Terry Barrera, Kate Maldonado, Dave Gutierrez, and Arturo Cuellar stood by me through thick and thin, from beginning to end- through stormy or sunny weather.

Marlon Jensen, a multi-faceted artist, provided the necessary guidance and assistance in the implementation of the entire photographic framework. This aspect of the project was necessary to bring life to the personal stories depicted throughout the document. I am grateful to him for his commitment to produce results that reflect a significantly high level of professional quality to the outcome. Most importantly, his willingness to become a significant part in the planning, preparation, editing, and completion of this endeavor, is heartfelt and deeply appreciated.

Author's note:

In some situations throughout this book, names have been changed to protect identity.

FOREWORD

We Pass This Way but Once

By Andy Porras

San Felipe. An original Hispanic Camelot. A legendary Latino barrio and idyllic locale, which for one brief, historical moment, brought great happiness and even glamorous ambience to its subjects. It may still yet prevail, but in the many memories of its subjects, it was engraved as a location that had high ideals. It was a place of excitement, purpose, and culture. Lots of culture. There, all was well, the wonderful life was grand. Yes, life was good in San Felipe. A place where we came together to celebrate our prosperity of acquired wisdoms and true happiness.

Our beloved high school campus was the heart of our Camelot and it was there that our dreams took their roots. It was also the very campus where I first met Dr. Tony Cavajal, well-known at the time as Los Onis.

We graduated, breaking our barrio bonds, and went out into another world to leave our mark. Dr. Carvajal's journey however, rivals any other work ever read by me. It offers a mirror image of what many of us had to endure and achieve in order to reach our specific goals. Our stories are so alike, yet so different- but so true.

In *The Roads We Traveled*, Dr. Carvajal's depiction of our wonderful jente (people), teachers, parents, relatives, siblings, friends, and classmates, brought life to their stories in this dazzling and mesmerizing work-of-art. The negative prejudicial personalities, even though hurtful and humiliating, are treated with a taint of forgiveness of bitter and unkind hearts.

The book is clearly separated into four parts. The reader will find that Part One, *The Way It Was*, addresses life and how it was during the early years- when our parents and grandparents arrived to the new country. Part Two, *The Way We Were*, provides a powerful glimpse of the joyful and exciting school years we experienced in San Felipe. Part Three, *The Way We are Today*, describes the goals and achievements that were reached by students from the beloved San Felipe High School. Finally, Part Four, *Significant Truths and Revelations*, summarizes some of the legal nightmares experienced by families and their children during the times that they were unwelcomed and rejected by the public school systems.

There are both, positive and negative, messages in each section. Because of this, the treatment of the subject matter beckons a different kind of intellectual understanding. Each passage of time in our lives was an important lesson. There are some of which we want to keep in our hearts forever and some that we wish to forget. Due to the complexity of our days, Dr. Carvajal presents the treatment of the subject matter with sensitivity and a hint of caring.

Throughout these pages, our lives are once again intertwined and become one voice, one thought, and one declaration: **We are San Felipe**- anywhere and anytime. After everything is said and done, it is possible that you may forget Del Río, but San Felipe will remain in your heart. Forever.

Andy Porras,
Sacramento, CA

PROLOGUE

Dave Gutierrez

This dry barren land stretches north across the border from central Mexico into west Texas. It extends across the southern portion of New Mexico and southeastern parts of Arizona. It is the unforgiving Chihuahua Desert. On the eastern tip of the desert, and three miles across the border, is the city of Del Río Texas. If not for the natural San Felipe springs that produce millions of gallons of water per day in Del Río, the desert border might continue even further into Texas.

It is believed that Spanish Missionaries gave a mass here in 1635 on St. Phillips Day, thus baptizing the area around the springs as San Felipe. Many who passed through the area saw it as an oasis around the barren land. Caves have been found with paintings and aboriginal art that date back 4,000 years before the birth of Christ.

James H. Taylor was born in Pennsylvania in 1832. By the age of twenty-eight, he owned and operated a large ranch in Uvalde, Texas- located some seventy miles west of the San Felipe springs. His Mexican wife, Paula Losoya Taylor, who was born in Guerrero Tamaulipas Mexico, was three years younger than James.

In 1862, cattle had been stolen from the Taylor Ranch. As the bandits were tracked near the Mexican Border, Paula and James stumbled across the vast water supply produced by the San Felipe springs. They quickly saw the potential in the land for development with the water supply. Along with Paula's sister, Refugia Losoya, they moved the family ranch to that area. They acquired the land by petitioning the government for a land grant. They hired locals to develop the land by building irrigation canals and became some of the founders of the city. James Taylor died in 1876, leaving all property and possessions to his wife, Paula.

The large land development project created many jobs and brought many from outside the area to get a taste of the profits to be had near the Taylor Ranch. A railroad station was built and in 1882 the first train rolled into town. The locals now needed a post office in the town they called San Felipe Del Río. A nearby town called San Felipe de Austin made things a bit confusing so the U.S. Postal Department had their name shortened to simply, Del Río.

Many local Mexicans were hired to do the work needed to build a growing town. As word reached Mexico, more arrived to find work and a living. The San Felipe Creek runs through the town and under the railroad tracks. The creek became the boundary of which separated the Anglos from the Mexicans, with the Mexicans literally on the other side of the tracks. The other side of the tracks was the barrio, the beloved San Felipe Barrio, of Del Río Texas.

The barrio, separated more by economic means of living than anything else, became the starting point in which Mexicans saw as el otro paise (the other country). The other country might as well have been another world to those who settled in the San Felipe Barrio. Very little was available to Mexican citizens under the rule of President Porfirio Diaz. Looking for opportunities to work and survive, they came across the border to barrios like San Felipe.

Santos Garza was born in 1881, just across the border from Eagle Pass, Texas- in Pierdas Negras, Mexico. His father arrived in Del Río in 1898, working for Paula Taylor. Santos worked as brick mason and also helped build homes and businesses in the San Felipe Barrio. He became involved with a theatrical drama group in the barrio called, *The Company*. While socializing with the drama company he met his wife-to-be, Jesusita Galindo. Santos and Jesusita married in 1901. The newlyweds both worked at a hotel as waiter and chambermaid.

Before 1910, Garza had started to own and operate his own business in the barrio. He is also credited with opening the first theatre in the barrio. As time went on, he even opened a general store called, La Ciudad de Mexico. The Garza family tenaciously made their start in the new world.

George Washington Brown had migrated to the Del Río area from North Carolina. He owned a square block of land in the barrio that he donated to the community. It would become known as Brown Plaza, or La Placita- to those in the barrio. The plaza was dedicated on Cinco de Mayo in 1908. Business buildings surrounded the square plaza that became the center point of the barrio. On evenings, the community gathered at La Placita to share the latest news and make new acquaintances. Festivals and celebrations continuously happened at La Placita. Cinco de Mayo and 16th of September were huge annual celebrations that always took place there.

James and Paula Taylor's vision had planted the seeds for a new and growing town. With a growing town, also came children and the need for schools. In 1890, the town of Del Río formed the Del Río Independent School District. The boundaries of the new school district ended at the railroad tracks and the San Felipe Creek, keeping those who lived in the barrio out of the district schools.

Seven years before the Del Río Independent School District was formed, the San Felipe Barrio Community had built a wooden structure that served as a small school in the barrio. Many of the children in the barrio were also taught in homes that served as escuelitas, (little schools). In 1908, the wooden structure was replaced with a new building as the school. The San Felipe Barrio was growing at a rapid pace. In 1909, a second school was built, known in the barrio as La Escuela Amarilla, the yellow school, simply because it was painted yellow.

By creating the boundaries of the new school district back in 1890, essentially kept the Mexicans out of the Del Río Independent School District. The City of Del Río and the San Felipe Barrio became two separate cities living under one city flag. The separation divided the two communities not only racially, but socially and economically as well.

Many in Mexico revolted against the Diaz Regime. With revolution in the air, Mexico was becoming a very unstable place to raise a family. As the violence and death tolls mounted, many escaped north to the United States. It is estimated that between 1910 and 1920, over a million Mexican nationals made their way into the United States, many of them landing in the border towns of Texas.

By 1928, the Del Río Independent School District had some serious debt issues. Their solution to their money problems was to annex parts of the San Felipe Barrio and take over the two operating schools. This would allow the city to tax those in the area that they would be taking over, adding new funds to the city. The school district wanted no part of the San Felipe Barrio when it drew up its original boundaries, but now they were looking to cash in on the tax opportunities the barrio provided. In June, the Del Río Independent School District annexed a great portion of the San Felipe Barrio.

Santos Garza had become not only a leader, but the one leader and voice for the people of San Felipe. The outraged Garza sought legal representation from Del Río Lawyer Walter Jones who asked for five hundred dollars as a retainer. Jones asked Garza who would make the payment. Garza replied, "Well, San Felipe of course." Jones then asked, "Just who is San Felipe?" Garza's reply was, "I am." He then proceeded to write Mr. Jones a personal check for the retainer and note for the remainder of his legal fees. The community would later help pay for legal fees.

The San Felipe Community was proud of its two schools. Yes, the schools were overcrowded but it was their schools that had been built by their own people. The schools had become part of civic pride in the barrio. They were absolutely furious that their schools would no longer be theirs. After a gut wrenching legal battle on November 7th, 1928, San Felipe won its injunction to stop the Del Río Independent School District from annexing a great portion of their community. The Del Río school district appealed the case. They lost the appeal as well. A large celebration ensued at Brown Plaza.

Nothing could prevent the Del Río school district from making another attempt at annexation of the San Felipe Community. Garza and the civic leaders of San Felipe had only one choice; to form their own school district. On September 7th, 1929, the San Felipe Independent School District was officially formed. It became the only school district in the state of Texas that was formed in a Mexican Barrio for Mexican children. Santos Garza was named President on the Board of Education for the San Felipe Independent School District. Also serving on the board, were other respected community leaders; Castulo Gutierrez, Pablo Flores, Adolfo Maldonado, Victor Vasquez Jr., Rodolfo Gutierrez, and Andres Cortinas.

Castulo Gutierrez had been the first mail carrier in the barrio and was instrumental in naming many of the streets in San Felipe. Rodolfo Gutierrez had become the first lawyer in the San Felipe Barrio.

The highest grade for education in the barrio was the 7th grade. If the children wanted to continue their education they had to cross the tracks and the San Felipe Creek to attend school in the Del Río Independent School District. The district had one high school building and two elementary school buildings. A fourth building was separated by the athletic field and reserved for the Mexican children that attended school in the Del Río Independent School District.

On January 7th, 1930, the Board of Education for the Del Río Independent School District ordered an election to be held to appropriate funds for school expansion. The expansion included the addition of five rooms to be added to the Mexican building on the campus. Parents, including Jesus Salvatierra, were outraged that the district was adding more rooms to the Mexican building, meaning that their children would continue to be segregated.

Salvatierra hired a lawyer, John L. Dodson, and on March 2, they filed a lawsuit against the school district. It became the first legal case in the state of Texas that was heard regarding the segregation on Mexican children in a local school district. Attorney Manuel C. Gonzales, a member of the League of United Latin American Citizens (LULAC), also joined the case for no fee. LULAC was looking to bring an end to the segregation of Mexican students in the state of Texas with this historic case in Del Río.

Rather than argue the difference in classrooms facilities between Mexican and Anglo children, they argued that the segregation itself was illegal. The state of Texas was using the "Separate but Legal" doctrine that was legitimized by the Supreme Court in 1896 to keep the black children segregated. This did not apply to Mexican Children, however throughout the state of Texas, Mexican children were often segregated.

On May 15, Val Verde County Judge Joseph Jones ruled in favor of Salvatierra. That decision, unfolded the spurious attempt that Del Río Independent School District was illegally separating the Mexican children from the Anglo children. Judge Jones ordered an injunction to stop the construction of the building on the campus. It was a landmark victory for Mexican Americans of Del Río, or so they thought.

The school district appealed the decision to the Court of Civil Appeals. The district claimed that the Mexican children were only separated because of two educational reasons. First, they claimed that many of the children could not speak English. Second, they claimed that most of the children were gone for a good portion of the year when their families would leave the area for migrant farm work.

Judge J. Smith ruled that the school district was operating within its administrating power to manage the educational matters as it saw fit. Since the segregation was not a racial issue but rather an educational issue, the judge ruled in the Del Río Independent School District's favor. The Mexican children continued to be separated in the school district.

After San Felipe established their own school district in 1929, the need for a high school was evident and thus became a priority. Within a year, with multiple efforts and resources, one was built. On December 13th, 1930, the pride of San Felipe was completed and dedicated. San Felipe High School opened its doors to the children of the barrio.

The San Felipe community might have had limited resources. However, the education of their children was always a top priority in the barrio since the day when the first wooden structure was built in 1883.

A new high school facility adorned the barrio. The educators who taught here influenced and inspired a generation of future educators, civic and political leaders. The children who passed through these doors would leave a lasting legacy for many to follow. The roads they would eventually travel, started in the classrooms of the San Felipe Schools.

PART ONE
The Way It Was

CHAPTER ONE

A New World Indeed

My educational experience began in a school known as *Our Lady of Guadalupe*, a Catholic school in Del Río, Texas- in the barrio of San Felipe. This is the place where I was baptized as; Antonio Lopez Carvajal, in the year of 1939. In fact, each of my siblings; Ramon, José, Maruca, Francisco, Raul, and Amparo were also baptized there. Each of us were originally enrolled at *Our Lady of Guadalupe Catholic School*. Two of my older siblings continued their Catholic education until the 8th grade. The rest of us were able to attend only first and second grades. During these two years, our education was focused on the importance of faith and respect for others.

Our Lady of Guadalupe Church

"Faith in God is the bread of life." We heard that every week at Mass. As the months progressed, the concept became a part of our daily prayers and the way we lived. It was a value instilled in me from a young age by my mother. Prayer became a necessary and sustaining factor in our lives.

I was around seven years old when my mother, Consuelo, or Chelito, as she was endearingly dubbed, decided to send three of us to the Catholic school. Religion and faith had always been a stronghold in my mothers' family. These were the gifts that gave our grandparents, and other families like them, the certainty that somehow their faith would always carry them through difficult times.

Mom, in particular, was very staunch in her faith. Nothing would shake her belief. She inspired us to believe the way she did. Because of this, Catholic education was the way we would be educated- guided by the loving grace of priests and nuns.

Because our dad's employment was sporadic, family income was unpredictable. His job as a house painter was seemingly tentative and Mom's tenacity could diligently save enough money to make whatever payments it took, to be accepted, and remain in the Catholic school. Each weekend she set out to sell many of her old clothes, old shoes, blankets, and furniture to a lady who bought and sold used goods. Even though she could have asked her father, Don Antonio, for a loan to pay the school tuition to the church, her self-respect and pride prevailed.

Watching mom on weekends carrying large bags to the lady's house, made me feel proud of her efforts. She was constantly doing something to prepare us for school. Whenever she spoke about the strict obedience expected of us in school, she made me realize that my days of freedom would soon be over. My days of sleeping by the river with my pony, climbing trees, swimming, and swinging from tree to tree, would soon be memories.

The dreaded day finally came when mom walked my brothers and me to be matriculated into *Our Lady of Guadalupe Catholic School*. When school began, we were to behave well. The dress code specifically required that boys wear khaki pants, shirts, and a black tie. Shoes could be any color. Tennis shoes were not acceptable. We each had the same satchels packed with pens, pencils, and notebooks.

When we arrived the following day, the nun in charge advised the new students that a definite code of behavior had to be respected. The boys were expected to be lined up on one side of the playground, and the girls on the opposite. The rules were also defined for other activities. Recess for boys was set at a different time than girls. We also ate lunch at different times. The girls were always first.

The following week we learned that we had to attend mass every morning before class. The nuns were always present to monitor. The boys sat on one side of the church and the girls on the other. The girls also wore the same color outfits. There were even certain requirements for the way they were allowed to wear their hair. The boys didn't have rules pertaining to their hair. They were simply expected to comb their hair as long as it was short and clean.

The first two weeks were terribly uncomfortable. The teachers were Catholic nuns who had evidently gone through this same routine when they were growing up. To them, enforcing the rigid rules and regulations on us was second nature.

When classes finally started, we were assigned schedules that would be part of our daily school responsibilities. Since we were only a total of 12 boys in the first grade, the boys had to prepare to serve as Altar Boys. Six boys would serve during the five days we attended school, and the other six, would serve at Sunday masses. We rotated every other week. No questions.

We had to attend Catechism classes on Saturday mornings to boot. It was a bit too much. I kind of felt sad for the priests and nuns. They actually had to live in their dorms twenty four hours a day. During Catechism classes we were told many times that if we really wanted to go to heaven, this was the way. I believed in heaven with all my heart, but it was at this point that I wondered if I would ever make it. It seemed to take a lot of work.

The first week, we went on a field trip to become acquainted with the church facilities. In contrast to my home, the Catholic church was elegant. It was decorated in gold and the altar was wrapped in blue and white silk, making it look like a huge cake with lots of icing. Every day, parishioners brought flowers for the altar. It was an awesome sight. It looked like heaven.

Amazingly, four of my teacher nuns were caring and thoughtful while two were not. I worked hard for the nuns that liked me, and did very little for the ones that were addicted to hitting our hands with a ruler if we even sneezed.

The weeks went by very slowly and at a very boring pace until Mother Superior came in and introduced herself as Sister Anna. She was lovely and had the smile and eyes of an angel. She smelled very clean. Every day she wore a long black dress and Rosaries that looked like marbles hanging all over the front of her dress. Her black shoes were shining like stars. I had tried shining shoes at La Placita with my older brother José, who earned a lot of money. I wondered if he and I could be hired to shine shoes at this school.

One morning, after mass was over, Sister Anna told us that she was assigned to be our music teacher. She spoke to us for ten minutes. Gracefully and quietly, she walked to the piano and started singing. She was an angel that someone dropped down to us from heaven. I did not want her to stop.

When Sister Anna stopped singing, she reached for her case and asked two girls to pass the sheet music to the other girls, and two boys did the same for the males. She asked both boys and girls to read the lyrics with her in unison. The third time she told all of them to sing with her by reading from the music sheets. After twenty minutes she stood up and applauded the students. She announced, "Now we have a new choir." On the way home I sang the first church song I had ever heard or sang.

During a very special month, Sister Anna organized a musical show for the parents. The name of the show was "My Grandfather's Clock." She assigned me the role of the grandfather while the rest of the boys were the numbers on the clock. She taught us how to dance to the movement of the clock. She was an amazing dancer that showed us how to move our heads and arms to the rhythm of the tune. I was amazed that she was allowed to move so gracefully.

Our Lady was a good school, with good teachers, and a very clean and good place to be. It felt safe. Even my days serving as an Altar Boy were special. I was beginning to understand how Jesus could come into our lives in such magical ways. I always felt close to him. I felt proud of my new life and also joyful that we had some Nuns that cared for us.

My brothers and my sister Maruca, were happy that they had found ways to like school, while staying close to Jesus. Mom was also very proud of us. Every Sunday we were actually up on time and ready for the 9 o' clock Mass. Mom always wore her favorite black dress with a long black scarf, and a large Rosary. She was a proud Mama. I even wondered if someday she would become a nun. She had pictures of saints in her room where she sometimes lit candles. I wondered if she prayed like the nuns did.

During those days, my dad's job - painting houses, had been reduced from seven days a week to only three days. Mom would not ask my grandpa to help with the tuition in spite of having less windfall. A few months later, she finally had to admit that she simply couldn't afford Catholic education anymore. The lack of funds to pay for the tuition was causing much turmoil in our lives. One day she asked Father Santos if he could waive the tuition for us. He quickly declined and warned her that not providing a Catholic education for her children was a sin. He stressed that the consequences were serious. That very day I felt something was very wrong. She grabbed us harshly, and started walking home in a flash. We didn't know mom could walk so fast, vocalize ugly words to herself, or get so angry. She was a woman of few words unless provoked by insult.

Mom continued taking us to mass. One miserable and ugly Sunday morning, when we walked in through the two elegant doors at the front entrance, the devil was waiting for us. One of the ushers approached mom and told her that we could no longer attend Mass because we had not paid the school fees. "Until you pay three weeks that you are behind, you cannot come back to this church, and your children cannot come back to school. You have to find somewhere else."

The usher told mom that if she could read, she should read the sign that clearly read, 'La Familia Carvajal esta excomuncada de la Iglesias Catolica de este dia en adelante'('The Carvajal Family, as of this day, is excommunicated from the Catholic Church.') The notice was signed by Father Santos and other families were also suspended.

Mom was not a person who could ever tolerate abuse or disdain from anybody. For half a moment I thought that she would beat the living hell out of the devil usher. She grabbed us without hurting us or saying a word to the person who owned the church. We were emotionally and spiritually hurt. I hurt because the guy at the front of the church took a lot away from us, at least it did from me. A seven year old cannot define or process indignation or betrayal.

The usher at the front of the church took something very important that was already a big part of me. He took Jesus from me. He took my dear Sister Anna, and her voice that came to us like an angel from heaven. I didn't realize that it would take almost a life time to forgive myself for trusting a church that had taken away my faith so selfishly. I realized then, that money did matter.

CHAPTER TWO

From River to Land They All Came to America

On the Monday following the fiasco at the church, my tyrant mother walked us to a different school. It was a bright yellow building, thus receiving the name, La Escuela Amarilla (The Yellow School). Mom was welcomed with open arms and a cup of coffee. We had chocolate and freshly baked rolls from the corner bakery.

Escuela Amarilla

The chaotic environment mimicked that of a three ring circus. Any child that was seven or eight years old was placed in the third grade classroom on the new second floor, which had just been completed.

I felt terribly uncomfortable wearing my church-issued khaki pants and shirt. Mom could not afford new cloths for me, so that's all I had to wear. At least I had managed to hide my black tie in my pocket.

Evidently, there were two schools in the area, both in a different barrio. I lived in La Placita Barrio (The Plaza Neighborhood). At one point, my school had been known as School #1. It was an unimpressive wooden shack until 1908. Later, it was replaced by a new structure with a second story, becoming known as Central School. By the time I was to go there, it had been given the name: Escuela Amarilla. I had heard my mom telling our neighbors that my dad helped with painting the very bright, yellow school. I proudly bragged that fact to anyone that would listen.

A photo of school mates at Escuela Amarilla with me directly beneath right window.

Since Escuela Amarilla was only about 200 steps from our home, I was destined to become a scholar at the school. I had wondered where the other school was located. Later, I leaned that the second school was first named School #2, paralleling the name of our School #1. It too was later given a different name and came to be known as: Escuela Calaveras (Skull School), because the road to the school was shared with a cemetery. It was a two-room structure that was built one year after Escuela Amarilla, in the year of 1909. Later, two more rooms were added.

A photo of school mates at Escuela Calaveras.

A surge of new students at each school was the talk of the town. The news was evident in every corner of the barrios; small grocery stores, rental facilities, and transportation were immediate needs of the growing population. You would think someone had struck gold or oil.

Increased enrollment in the schools came from immigrants and refugees from the Mexican Revolution during the second decade of the twentieth-century, as well as from migrant families who were unable to return to Mexico.

About five-hundred students attended the first or second grade. By the time I was transferred to the third grade after leaving the Catholic school, the first and second graders that had arrived earlier, were now also entering the third grade.

Mom, who was panicked by the situation, immediately and assertively, enrolled us at the Escuela Amarilla, filled out all necessary forms and signed the papers. The next day she took us to school on the day classes started, kissed us goodbye, and told us to behave. She assured us that she would bring lunch to us.

The next day turned out to be quite freakish. This classroom, instead of my usual classroom of 12 boys, held a total of 45 boys and 32 girls. The girls were on one side of the crowded room and the boys on the other. We all sat side by side, in front of, or behind someone else. Either way we were stacked like sardines.

Recess time was a breath of relief. The entire school went outside at once. The ocean of kids poured out aimlessly from one side of the school to the other, all of them letting off of some steam.

I spent my time climbing one of the few trees that framed the rear side of the school. It was my sanctuary. It seemed that from the first time we chose to climb a certain tree, we owned it. It was a safe tree.

My tree was occupied by four students. Two students had just arrived from Mexico; Arturo Cuellar and Adan, another by the name of Rogelio, who wouldn't tell us where he came from, and me, who was born and baptized in America. We would spend the entire recess time on the tree while our teachers recovered from oxygen deprivation.

My mother came from Mexico with my grandparents, who also came to the United States of America during the Mexican Revolution. It seemed that my tree was shared by people, mostly from Mexico. I wondered if other climbers on top of the other trees also came from Mexico. Most of them did.

We didn't talk to each other. We rambled on and on in Spanish about almost anything, though we didn't listen to each other. Perhaps that was cultural. Every one of us talked at the same time. We tried to isolate words in Spanish, and even pretended that we knew words in English, which we often heard from our teachers.

During one of our rambling sessions on top of our tree, Adan said to me, "you silly boy." I responded, "Porqué silly?" ("Why silly?"). Arturo, another member of the tree, told Adan, "no le digas silly" ("do not call him silly"). Arturo was one of those kids nobody would mess with, and I mean **no**body. He was ready to push Adan off our tree. I felt good. Arturo seemed like a friend I needed just in case someone ever decided to try and beat me up. Adan was sad and scared.

I didn't like Adan because of his name. When I was in Catholic school, our teacher nuns told us that the reason we were sinners was because of a guy by the name of Adan who had a girlfriend by the name of Eva. She told him to take a bite from an apple she probably stole from a snake. He was stupid enough to take a bite from the green apple without permission from God. The story goes on to explain how Adan and Eva are responsible for making all of us sinners. I felt sorry for Adan, because he was stuck with such a name. I always wondered if Adan climbed our tree to make us sinners. Why in the world would a mother name her son by that terrible name?

When recess was over, we descended from our tree and we walked back to class together. Arturo and Adan happened to be sitting next to each other, all the way in the back of the room. I looked back and they were both laughing. After that day, we started using words in English, even if we didn't know what they meant.

One gloomy day Adan told me, "Don't be silly." Adan laughed. He was proud that he could speak English. Arturo stopped him and told him not to call me silly. Adan went on teasing me, "silly, silly Antonio, silly, silly boy." He knew what Arturo would do to him so he jumped off the tree and dashed away to be with the other 200 kids.

I later told Arturo that the word silly, meant funny. That was all. Arturo responded, "Ya basta" ("enough already"). He went on to say, "This is the deal. No one calls you silly. I don't like that word. Only goats are silly." "Perhaps not surprisingly, the word *silly* became one of my favorites. I still don't know exactly what it means. I use it often regardless. I frequently say to my grandkids, "Don't be silly."

Interestingly, my teacher's name was Mrs. Sunshine Humphrey. It was a name I thought was the name of a pastel (a pie), probably because sweet bread from the local bakery was a snack I always craved. We often had sweet bread for breakfast, lunch, and dinner. The name we used, when referring to her, was *Sunshine*. It was an easy name to remember, even though she did not have the persona of a sunshine person. She was actually rather strict, cloudy, and firm.

I am certain that Mrs. Sunshine felt trapped- probably more out of fear and discomfort of having to deal with 99.9% of the monolingual, Spanish-speaking students. English was her one and only language. I predict that her new reality was beyond appalling to see so many kids that spoke absolutely nothing but Spanish.

Escuela Amarilla had no dress codes. Each of us wore what we had. I wore my khaki outfit two months in a row. Arturo finally asked me if I had anything different to wear. I told him that was a *silly* question. Surprisingly, he did not react to the word *silly* as I had been anticipating. I told mom that all the kids were making fun of my uniform, so she bought me a new shirt- to shut me up.

My mother, along with other parents, usually arrived thirty minutes earlier than school was to be dismissed, seeking to have an after school conference with the teachers, desiring to review homework assignments and discipline problems. They had no such luck. There was no feasible way the teachers could make enough time to stay after school to answer questions to an army of parents.

CHAPTER THREE

Mañana de Carnaval
(Morning of the Carnival)

Children and parents from La Calaveras Barrio managed to walk or find transportation for themselves when they had to get to La Placita Barrio. La Placita became their social outlet; their carnival, their music, and their appreciation for life- especially when cultural celebrations were scheduled to start.

La Placita

When the peacefulness of my barrio was about to change, I always knew it ahead of time. It was obvious to me three weeks before the commotion even started. I heard the hammering of booths being erected, platforms being built, and witnessed businesses being painted or cleaned throughout La Placita.

During the beginning of each September, while my neighbors around La Placita prepared for the grand festivities of the *16th of September* celebration, sleep never came easy for me. There were sounds of whining and yelping dogs, cats getting into fights, and cries from my determined pony, Jackie. Jackie called out for his mother, wishing to return to her across the river banks. The constant hammering noises that exploded across the street from La Placita, were enough to induce a seemingly-permanent inability to reach any level of peace.

I could never understand how the rest of my brothers and sisters managed to ever-so-gracefully, slip into slumber in our crowded bedroom. We shared our room with two dogs, six cats, and my sister's endearing lamb, Nikibungeray (Nikki-Boong-Gur-Ray). Even Jackie, tried desperately to force himself through the kitchen door to join us in the crowded bedroom even though it would prove impossible. Mom would often patrol the entrance, blocking the door with the kitchen table or anything else she could find. After several attempts, Jackie realized that he was not welcome.

I could not comprehend how musicians managed to be so alert and ready to construct their personal stages, while also dedicating time to practice the songs they had planned for the festivities. Somehow, they must have managed to find secluded areas by the river to practice the difficult songs they were attempting to learn, only a few days prior. One of the traditional ballads, *Cielito Lindo*, was a song my mother had learned to sing and play with artistic finesse on her mother's piano when she was a young girl.

After hearing the jubilant notes of *Cielito Lindo*, even the dogs and my grandmother's parrot would bark and sing to the memorable tune and lyrics; "canta y no llores, porqué cantando se allegran cielito lindo los corazones"("sing and don't cry because singing makes the hearts and the heavens fill with joy").

Besides enjoying the daily repertoire of piano music, I was always amazed at how my mother Chelito, her sister Amparo, and my aunt Carolina managed to follow the complex recipes they had each concocted. They did so while still being able to complete a variety of kitchen tasks, dictated by my grandma Doña Panchita, and with amazing diligence.

My abuelita and abuelito: Doña Panchita
and Don Antonio Ramirez

My abuelita (grandmother), Doña Panchita, came with my abuelito (grandfather), Don Antonio, from Sonora, Mexico. They had escaped the Mexican Revolution. She knew the science and the art of preparing, cooking, and serving unique and authentic Mexican dishes. These exquisite dishes were also produced for the September celebrations, at her diner across La Placita.

Grandma's diner was a special place with a variety of menu items. Some unique entrees included; Cabrito (Goat), Chile Rellenos (Chile and cheese stuffed burritos), caldo de res y pollo (beef broth and chicken), and higado (liver). Such were the specialty plates- well known for their flavorful taste. All of the meats and vegetables were home grown. Her diner was attended by business people from Del Río- the city across the barrio, who came, simply to enjoy a special dining experience for lunch or dinner.

Theatrical performers, musicians, and other professionals from nearby places in Mexico or from as far as San Antonio, came to savor the amazing cuisine prepared by Doña Panchita's team while enjoying the musical atmosphere. Even though the kitchen is now closed after eighty years, her home is known today as a museum; preserved as Casa de La Cultura (House of Culture). To this day, visitors continue to attend artistic, musical activities and lectures presented there once a month.

During days of celebration, La Placita was adorned by booths trimmed with red, white, and green to commemorate the pride and significance of Mexico prevailing in a battle against Spain. Each year, the entire Mexican community, who had settled at different barrios in San Felipe, always found a purpose and ways to celebrate using La Placita for weddings, birthdays, and special religious holidays.

Music, dance and jubilant excitement continued for any and every reason the community could justify. For many of us growing up in La Placita or the Calaveras barrios, we did not find it necessary to determine or define any specific purpose for the glitter, exuberance, or joyful songs and dances.

CHAPTER FOUR

Tempest in a Teapot

With the passing of years, La Placita lost some its glitter and its gentry. Less than a block away from the place where so much joy had happened in our lives, various unhappy changes were about to take place in my own family. My siblings and I knew something was terribly wrong with my mom and dad. Each night seemed to be worse than the night before. Some days were somber and deadly quiet, and other days the war between them escalated enough to incite fear in us. Either way, our lives were changing for the worse.

Mother became gradually more intolerant of my dad's alcohol abuse, eventually leading to verbal and physical violence. In this case, mom was the dominant one. On his way home, dad would spend time at the corner Cantina with co-workers, who shared work as house painters of expensive homes in the Anglo neighborhoods. When he later arrived at home, my dad would meekly weave himself to a back room that was adjacent to the house. He would always ask me to walk with him for support. There he would cry and argue quietly before falling asleep. I felt important to be his friend and to be there when he needed me.

Mom was going through her own private hell. Within a single year, she had to go through surgery for breast removal, gave birth to my premature brother, and lost her mother, my grandmother Panchita- the love of our lives.

Around the same time, my dad received a notice from the U.S. Military, informing him that he was ordered to appear at a recruitment office to process necessary papers needed for entrance to the Military

Service. Among other requirements, he had to be present for a complete physical examination.

Within a few weeks, my dad was informed that he had a severe form of Pulmonary Tuberculosis and was not eligible for the service. Our mother was in complete shock. Soon after, during a very warm day, dad collapsed while painting a two story home on the other side of town. A close friend of my father, Felix Cardenas, drove to our home and briskly informed us that dad was at the Val Verde hospital and was very sick. Mom frantically left in the car with Mr. Cardenas.

When Felix and my mother entered the hospital, she was told to wait until Dr. Hyslop could see her. Within an hour, Dr. Hyslop arrived and informed mom that my dad was very sick and needed x-rays. They kept my dad overnight. The next day, all of us went back with mom to see dad. Mom was worried and totally distraught.

Before noon, Dr. Hyslop confirmed to mom that the physical report from the military, was true. Dad had a severe condition known as Tuberculosis. He firmly cautioned mom that the condition was very common in the area and was extremely contagious and incurable. Dependent upon the home-care dad could get, the doctor predicted dad would have less than nine months to live. The doctor was very insistent that none of us, except mom, should ever be anywhere near him. If we were, we would get the infection within days.

Before dad was dismissed from the hospital all of us were sent to live with our aunt Manina, except for our two older brothers. I never knew where they went. Our days were dreadfully lonely without our dad.

Mom was a valiant "nurse-on-duty," twenty four hours a day. She would bathe and feed her husband and disinfected his clothes in boiling water. During this difficult time, she seemed to be preparing herself for the inevitable. We were allowed to see dad, but only from a distance as he walked around the backyard in his blue striped pajamas, that he always liked. I just wanted to run to him when he waved at us.

That was the way our days were until our dad succumbed to Tuberculosis. The miserable, infectious, and contagious disease that ran rampant in those days, had finally taken him. Due to the nature of the illness, none of us were allowed to be near him during his last days. We were not even permitted to attend the burial.

He died on my eleventh birthday. Raul and Francisco were two years younger than I. My sister Magdalena was thirteen and our youngest sister, Payito, was two years old. Our two older brothers endured their agony on their own, wherever they were. Our father's departure was very difficult for both of them. José, especially, never seemed to recover from losing dad.

My father, Ramon, and my mother, Consuelo

CHAPTER FIVE

Pain and Healing Changes Everything

Twelve months after the funeral, mom had successfully completed the entire year of Luto (mourning), dictated as a Mexican custom for women. During this time mom wore only black dresses.

Our abuelito, Don Antonio Ramirez, who had been absent for a few months, returned to see us. He had been disappointed to see mom struggle with my dad's unacceptable lack of family responsibilities. We had been missing his weekly treats of nickels for gum or candy. He was a man of few words, when it came to us and our mother. During a very somber Saturday morning, he asked us to walk to La Placita, so he could spend some time with his daughter.

Before leaving for our long and brisk walk, mom stooped close to us and told us not to go too far. Like a commanding army officer, she firmly stated that we had to learn to listen to her when she told us to do something. We had to be responsible for ourselves now that our father was gone.

For the very first time, we noticed that our mother was missing most of her front teeth. Her hair also seemed to have fallen out in chunks. Perhaps the years struggling to make our days tolerable without dad, had resulted in the person we saw before us. We had vague memories of the way she used to be. Pictures of her from her younger days hadn't given any warning of what her latter deterioration and suffering would do to her. The days when she used to dance, sing, and play the piano seemed to be part of another life.

Three weeks later, grandpa informed us that Mom was going to a hospital in Ciudad Acuna, Mexico to fix her teeth and her crooked jaw. He asked us to take care of each other with the help of our aunt Manina. He explained to us that when mom returned from her hospital stay, she would have to rest and was not be bothered by any of us.

Grandpa promised us a train ride to San Antonio as our reward for helping mother get better. That's all he said, but proved true to his word. Our train ride to San Antonio was magical. I had never seen so many cows eating grass as I witnessed throughout the trip. When we arrived in San Antonio, our grandpa corralled us onto a bus.

Soon enough, we had arrived at a very nice hotel. Two of us were assigned to a room with very clean towels, soap, and new clothes. Our meals were served at the hotel diner, where we'd eat, before visiting the grandest places in the city. We spent five days there. On the last day, he took us to church, before we headed home. He bought each of us the most spectacular souvenirs we had ever possessed.

When we arrived home our mother was playing a piano she had rented with money she had earned working part time at *Kress*, a department store. Our living room was decorated with flowers and accented with embroidered place mats that were made by Aunt Caro. When we entered to investigate where the sweet tunes were coming from, we saw a beautiful and happy woman that we had never seen before. It was our mom with a totally new set of teeth and new hair. She was proud, holding her head up high with elegant and radiant beauty.

Mother had rediscovered an appreciation for her life and her well-being, and we discovered the importance and power of external family, which created an immense support system for us. We realized that we were not captives anymore and were now free to wander away from our home and reconnect with cousins, aunts, and uncles.

I exercised my newfound freedom to wander around. I spent many mornings climbing my tree, fishing, and swimming in my river. Two Anglo boys had become frequent visitors that I was quite used to seeing during those mornings. They used to jump to the shallow parts of my river and walk across to climb the trees with me. This went on for several weeks until the infamous day that an angry woman came.

The woman yelled at the kids to get their "asses" home as quickly as possible. I looked down from my tree and saw a red-haired woman coming close to the river bank. She was screaming to the kids, "Get over here! How many times have I told you not to play with that dirty Mexican?" I wondered if the crazy lady was talking about me. I refused to believe that I was dirty. I was always very clean from swimming in my river all day long; hour after hour.

I witnessed her beating my friends with a stick, while screaming in an angry and demanding way. She continued pointing at me on my tree. When I realized that I was the dirty boy she was talking about, I thought she would also come after me. I quickly scampered off to tell my mom. In my desperation, I could not articulate the incident. I finally attempted to tell mom that the red-hair bruja (witch), that lived across the river, had told my little friends that they could not play with me anymore because… "Callate!" ("Shut up!") Mom interrupted me suddenly and firmly, wishing to hear no more. I knew I was going to miss the two Anglo boys and the peanut butter jelly sandwiches they used to share.

CHAPTER SIX

The Sun Also Rises

I had an army of cousins and friends who ended up compensating for the loneliness of our otherwise empty days. As time progressed, several clusters of families became integrated into our family circle; the Rodriquez family, from my mother's side, and the Carvajal family, from my father's.

My dad had five siblings; Juan, Francisco, Vicente, Adolfo, and Refugia a.k.a. Cuca. His mother's name was Inocente. She was born in Jimenez, Coahuila, Mexico on December 28th, 1878 and died on May 19th, 1947. My grandfather's name was Felix Carbajal. He was born on December 18th, 1870, in San Antonio, Texas, and died on July 11th, 1960.

Felix and Inocente Carbajal

Due to their proximity to our home and the ages of their children; Juan, Caro, Vicente, and Guadalupe, were available to assist our mother whenever emergent situations occurred. Vicente and Guadalupe had two boys, cousin Vicente Jr. and Armando, who were also ready to help my mother in any way that she needed. Both families lived near the Escuella Amarilla, which was only a few blocks from us.

Vicente and Guadalupe Carbajal

Juan and Carolina (Caro) Carvajal, had four daughters together; Catalina (later nick-named Kate), Dora, Estela and Nina. My sister Maruca (who adopted the Anglo name, Maggie) and Kate were very close cousins. They were both the same age. Estela was my age, so naturally, she and I also became good friends. Dora and Nina both married young and therefore, were not socially close to us. Juan, my uncle and his wife Tia (Aunt) Caro had been significant advocates for my mother during my dad's illness. They provided meals for her and brought her his medical prescriptions from the local pharmacist, Señor Hernandez, for the entire duration that she was focused on her husband's care.

Aunt Caro and her daughters

Kate was the eldest of the four daughters. When World War II ended, she was eleven years old. She shared her feelings, with enormous pride, when the end of the war was announced at last. It was a glorious day when she heard the church bells ringing continuously to give thanks to our Lord for fulfilling his promise to bring our soldiers home.

However, many men from our barrio did not return. The Carvajal's who had gone to war, returned on *D-Day*. Though shattered in spirit, from having seen the brutal twelve-year, Holocaustic, Nazi tyranny in concentration camps, they were thankful to be home.

Our Lady of Guadalupe church and other local churches were packed with people expressing gratitude for those who returned. Of those who did not return, some were prisoners or missing in action, some of which would later be declared dead.

The 1945 Conquistador, our school year book, was dedicated to our heroes from San Felipe and the memory of their loved ones; "Greater love hath no man than this, that a man lay down his life for his friends. John 15:33."

The ugly truth, was that when our boys; our Heroes, returned from the war, they were not allowed to walk on the main streets or enter public facilities in the city. Their dedication to the city was betrayed by signs that read: "Whites Only." The blatant racism in the city of Del Río, against anyone who was not white, was at its worse.

After the death of our father, the Juan Carvajal family became a surrogate family for my siblings and me. My aunt Carolina provided a strong amount of stoic support for us. Mother had always valued the trust and confidence that she and Caro had for each other, even during our most difficult years.

Because of the variance in age between my siblings and Caro's daughters, I had benefited greatly by staying close to my cousin Estela. She and I were both the same age and thus, were also in the same grade throughout high school. Estela became my mentor and my monitor. She guided me well towards the safety nets of social life. She and Maggie would conspire and decide where I would go and with whom. Each week before the weekend finally arrived, they would ordain the various events and activities that I could attend or participate in.

Over the years, Kate had been blessed. She evolved as a professional artist, just like her dad. She started painting at the early age of five. She developed and honed her own techniques at that age. First, she began painting with oils and water colors. Her magnificent productions went on to include the use of pastels, acrylics, and charcoal.

Most of Kate's works are done in oils. My favorite piece, was a painting of *Our Lady of Guadalupe*, surrounded with roses. This masterpiece was created on a material for a chasuble, which she presented as a surprise to Reverend Roberto Peña, O.M.I., at St. Joseph's Catholic Church. Kate's works have always reflected her amazing imagination, which was inspired by the works of the greatest masters in the world of art. She loved to read the art classics of Leonardo De Vinci, Michelangelo, and Diego Rivera.

In her spare time today, Kate totally and completely spoils her grandchildren, which includes two sets of twin boys. She and her late husband, Santana Maldonado, have three children; Dr. Rolando Maldonado, Roberto Maldonado, and Linda M. Fenton. Rolando is a physician, Roberto is a law enforcement officer, and Linda is a teacher for the San Antonio School District.

Kate and one set of the Fenton twins"

Another family cluster was the Raul (Payino) and Amparo (Manina) Rodriguez family. Their family was very dear to us during the most difficult years after our dad had died. They had four daughters; Teresita, Berta, Francisca, and Mary. They also had a son by the name of Raul Jr. whom had died from a freak accident, during a football practice, when he was just a freshman in high school.

The Rodriguez girls then and now

In many ways, our entire extended family became very strong advocates for all of us. Due to difficult financial and emotional burdens, both Payino and Manina also became our surrogate parents. They took loving care of us in their home while mom was recovering from the death of her husband, our beloved father.

Payino and Manina: Raul and Amparo Rodriguez

I was fascinated at the early beginnings of my uncle, Raul Rodriguez (Payino), and his struggle to escape from Sonora, Mexico. He came to the United States of America in a box car that was used for cattle. His dad, mother, and the rest of his family arrived in similar ways, surviving their passage to Texas- alive and ready to start a new life.

Payino's mother was a talented seamstress in San Buena Ventura, in the state of Coahuila, Mexico. She brought her gift to Del Río where she easily managed to become a well-known and respected seamstress in the barrio. Payino's father, Don Vicente, was an accomplished carpenter in Mexico. He too, carried his carpentry skills with him to the new world we knew as San Felipe. No time was wasted. He quickly became a well-known carpenter; building homes and making fine assortments of cabinets, chairs, and other admirable hand-carved items.

Payino was no stranger to creative efforts either. I remember him as extremely conscientious, dedicated, and versatile in his work. He could tackle any challenge and confront whatever obstacles he would encounter. He was a rather noble and genuine uncle, who always encouraged me to take my studies seriously. Through the years, I admired their unrelenting dedication and support for other families who came from Mexico. Their generosity seemed limitless.

Manina played a special role in the Rodriguez family. Every member of her household member knew that well. With a household of over ten people, only a person with a determined disposition like Manina, could coordinate the responsibilities of the family. She was even in charge of providing toilet training for one of her seven cats. She was the Commander in Chief. In the evenings, before I was ready to go to bed, she would review the homework assignments I had to submit the next day. I did not dare to disappoint her.

I knew and respected Manina's commitment to work and her undying resilience. Several times, while mom was on the verge of giving birth to one of my siblings at home, I would run in a panic to get Manina…or scamper up a tree. After Manina arrived, knowing very well the protocol of the next agonizing moments, I prayed to Jesus that mom would hurry up with her pain and be done with whatever bothered her. Manina had assisted my mother with the birthing of four of my younger siblings which brought clarity to my understanding of where we came from.

The day Payito was to be born, Manina ordered all of us to go the river and to our trees and wait until she called for us. The experience mom was about to endure, I already knew, was known as Labor. Laborious it was. When Payito was finally born, she announced to the world that she was angry and very hungry. Manina was indeed a tender, loving, and super-nurse. The doctor was summoned to clip the umbilical which he later charged $15.00 for. It wasn't like he had to do anything. My mother and Manina had done all of the hard work.

My brothers, sisters, and I had been taken care of, through the amazing generosity of our families. When the birthing was done, we returned home from our river hideaway to fend for each other as a family.

Mom secured a full time position at *Kress* in the candy department. She walked across the bridge for work at 8 a.m. and did not return until 6 p.m. She appointed Maggie and me to act as guardians for our siblings. Our aunts, Manina and Caro, were assigned as secondary emergency systems. Both were willing to be on call if they ever heard that we had been swimming in the river twenty yards away from our house without their permission.

A surveillance system was never required. We knew how to take care of each other. The care system included each of my cousins, their friends, and each of us. When we combined Payito, Raul, Francisco, Magdalena and I, along with all of our friends, we had a full blown army of more than ten confident and competent swimmers. When we added other cousins and neighbor friends to the mix, we had a ready-made infantry of over thirty soldiers.

We spent our days emulating the bravery of Tarzan along with his son, Boy, and the beautiful Jane. They came alive from the Saturday matinees we saw each week on the silver screen. There was no way on God's green earth that we could ever let mom find out that we spent at least eight hours in the river, in trees, or basking in the sun.

Twice daily, three different tree scouts had the obligation to climb the tallest trees possible and swing from vine to vine to alert the rest of us that the coast was clear. Two hours before mom would return, everyone scampered off to their own homes. We dried the towels on top of bushes in the hot sun, cleaned the house, and rested peacefully to welcome mom as she walked inside. Even our mascot, Jackie, seemed to understand our sophisticated strategy. Mom would warm the dinner she had prepared in the morning before she left for work. She expressed appreciation to God for the very fine children she was blessed with.

There was another Carbajal family that lived close to us. Refugia (Cuca) and Luis Martinez Sr. had three children; Gilberto, Edmundo, and Elia. Refugia had a second marriage to Genaro Moran. They raised a child by the name of Genaro Moran Jr. Genaro Jr. married Hilda Sanchez and stayed in San José, California. Elia, stayed in Del Río and lived in La Placita Barrio, very close to our river. She married Mario Barragan Sr.

Elia

Elia attended *Our Lady of Guadalupe* Catholic school from grades one through eight. She went on to *Sacred Heart Academy*, where she graduated in 1940. For a short period of time, Elia moved to California to work in the fruit canaries. She later returned to Del Río, Texas, where she married Mario Barragan Sr.

Elia worked for the San Felipe School District as a teacher's aide in the mid 1960's. She eventually started attending night school. Her efforts resulted in a positive and well-earned reward. She completed her Bachelor's Degree at *Sul Ross State University* in 1981.

Elia utilized her well-earned degree by teaching the 2nd grade at *Stephan F. Austin*, *Garfield*, and *East Side Elementary*. Her teaching career began in 1982 and she taught until she retired in 2004. Mario worked at Las Novedades in advertising. Later he worked for the Alcoholic and Beverage Commission at the International Bridge. Mario later retired from the Texas Department of Agriculture.

Picture of Mario and Elia dancing

Mario Sr. presently resides in Del Río, Texas. His and Elia's daughter, Gladis, lives in Santa Rosa, California. Their son, Mario Jr. and his wife, Celia Siguero, live in New Braunfels, Texas. Mario and Celia were married on November 12th, 1977. They have two children; Maricela and Mario Armando. Maricela is married to Jeremy Gaytan and lives in Arkansas. Mario Armando married a woman named Jessica Fernandez. They live in New Braunfels and have two girls; Absedy and Sophia.

Mario Jr., Celia, and their grandchild, Sophia-
one of Mario Amando's daughters

Mario Jr. and Celia's children;
Mario Amando and Maricela Gaytan

My parents, Ramon and Consuelo lived in a compound that belonged to my grandparents, Don Antonio and Doña Panchita Ramirez. The huge plot was separated into three sections. We lived in one house, my aunt Manina and uncle Payino lived in another, while my abuelito and abuelita lived in the third section.

My grandparents were very fortunate to have settled so near La Placita when they migrated from Mexico. They strove to make a living by purchasing a building which they remodeled and converted into a successful restaurant.

The restaurant sat near the river, had beautiful gardens of magnolias and bougainvilleas, and of course, served excellent food. The setting of the restaurant was so picturesque that musicians and actors, from various places in Mexico and the United States, came to enjoy the ambience.

My mom and dad had seven children. Their five boys were given the names; Ramon, José, Franciso, Raul, and Antonio (me). Their two daughters were named Maruca and Amparo. Maruca would adopt the Anglo names Magdalena and Maggie, while Amparo briefly took on the name Amy, but was known as Payito for most of her life.

Ramon graduated from San Felipe High School in 1949. After graduation, he enlisted in the Air Force. After he returned from serving four years in the military, he enrolled and completed a Bachelor's degree in Electrical Engineering at *Southern Methodist University* (SMU) in 1957. He went on to complete his Master's degree in Business at the *University of North Texas* in 1967. Ramon died in 1978.

Ramon's wife, Mary Ellen, received an Associate Degree from *Richland College*, in 1988. Ramon and Mary Ellen had three daughters who all currently live in Texas. Each of them attended and completed degrees from the same universities that Ramon attended. Ramon's three daughters had the names; Elena, Anna, and Laura.

My brother, Ramon

Elena Carvajal earned a Bachelor's degree in English, at the *University of North Texas*, in 1979. Master's in Library Science, *University of North Texas* in 1980.

Tony and Elena (Gigi), with their daughter Sophia

Anna Carvajal earned a Bachelor's degree in Political Science at the *University of Texas* in Dallas. To date, she has earned 30 credit hours towards a Juris Doctorate at *Texas Tech*.

Marc, Anna, and their son, Jacob

Laura Carvajal obtained a Bachelor's degree and then a Masters degree in Economics, at SMU. Her MBA is currently in progress.

Magdalena Carvajal, my dear Maruca, currently lives in San José, California. Maggie attended *San José City College* and completed a business certificate. After her training at *Junior College* she attended the Institute for Business and Technology. After completion of the program, she was employed by the Asthma and Allergy Center for four years and then ABC Pediatrics, for three years.

After seven years in the medical system, Maggie was assigned to a position as an office manager for a medical group in San José, California for twenty years, until she retired. After her retirement, Maggie chose the most important role in her life- she became the pillar of strength and steadfast support in the lives of several grand and great grandchildren.

Maggie's years of wisdom and experience brought her great focus in guiding and inspiring her grandchildren to appreciate the importance of self-discipline, self-respect, and realizing the value of an education. She is the emotional rock of support who is always available for their needs.

Maggie played a significant role in the lives of family and friends alike, which was well affirmed at her 80th birthday celebration in San José, taking place on December, 24. 2014. Maggie's popularity goes on and on. So does her love for friends and family.

Maruca / Magdalena / Maggie: Then and now

Two of Maggie's Grandchildren; Junior and Allysa

José Carvajal (Joe) graduated from San Felipe High School in 1952. Joe was the central-most source of support for our family after our father passed away. He maintained jobs on weekends and weekday evenings, while completing the last years of high school.

Joe's, forte was sports. He was a *Golden Gloves* champion and an avid football player. He was an industrious individual with an admirable and strong work ethic. He pushed me hard, inspiring me, as well as the rest of my brothers and sisters, to take our obligations in life seriously.

After high school, Joe attended *San Marcos College* on a football scholarship, which was no surprise to any of us. After two years, he joined the United States Army. He was honorably discharged after two years of service.

Joe married his high school Sweetheart, Dora Garcia, who graduated from San Felipe High School the same year that he did. They had three children; Joe Jr., Mario, and Belinda. José passed away in 2006.

José and Dora

Fransisco and Raul looked like twins. Everywhere one of them went, the other was sure to follow. When Fransisco insisted on attending school in San José, California, instead of in San Felipe, the Raul followed. They were together until they graduated from *James Lick High School*. It was at this juncture that they went their separate ways. Francisco joined the Army and was stationed in Germany for two years. Ironically, Raul also joined the Army and went to Vietnam for two years. After they returned, each of them found their own goals in life.

Raul attended The University of Northern Colorado and earned a Bachelor's degree in Sociology. After his degree, he obtained a position as a therapist in a family mental health agency, where he worked for five years. Later on, he worked for the U.S. Postal Service for twenty six years until his retirement. Raul was married. He has two loving daughters; Cynthia and Christina, who remain a significant part of his life.

Francisco worked for Hewlett Packard Corporation in California until his retirement. He and his wife Grace, had three children; Francisco Jr., Aaron, and Cassandra.

Amparo (Amy) Carvajal Rosen was the dearest of the family. This was because she was the youngest one in the family, and a sweet girl to boot. Her adorable ways earned her placement on the pedestal of love by her family. We nick named her Payito until she received a Master of Science degree in Nursing from Washington University.

Amparo and Sheldon Rosen had three children; Raquel, Nicolas, and Annie. Their girls are gifted musicians in violin and piano. Nicholas is a professional surfer and painter. Annie, the violinist, competed a Bachelors of Art degree from *Pitzer College* in Carlton, California and Raquel completed a Bachelor's degree with two double majors; Near Eastern Languages and Civilization (NELC) and International Studies Jewish Studies, with double minors in Comparative Islamic Studies and Comparative Religion.

Raquel and Annie Rosen with cousin
Cynthia in the center

The Carvajal Family; Tony, Raul, José (Joe),
Amparo (Payito), and Maruca (Maggie)

Antonio, Joanie, and daughter Jennifer

Joanie and I married in 1969, in Greeley, Colorado. Joanie's parents were from De Moines, Iowa. My mother, Consuelo was born in Monterrey, Mexico and my father, Ramon, was born in Del Río, Texas.

Joanie has been a nurse in the Intensive Care Cardiology Unit for thirty years, and I am now retired from the field of Education after Forty two years. I completed a Bachelors of Science degree in English and

Speech at *Sul Ross University*, my Master's degree in Special Education and Sociology at Texas A&M University, and finally, my Doctorate in the College of Education and Behavioral Sciences at the University of Northern Colorado. Post-Doctoral education was completed at Stanford University and Betty Ford Clinic in Rancho Mirage, California.

I passionately continue my professional life as a Writer. I have published two other books; *Essential Moments* and *Embraced by Love*. This book was published in June of 2015. I have served as an International consultant in North Africa in the provinces of: Tunisia, Gabes, Sfax, Jerba, and Timbactu. I've also consulted in Ireland, Spain, Ecuador, Novascotia, and at numerous universities and public schools in the United States of America.

Joanie and I have three wonderful children; Jennifer Carvajal Kabacy, Carmela Carvajal Kim, and Marc Anthony. Marc and Jennifer live in Seattle, Washington and Carmela resides in San Francisco, California.

Jennifer completed a Bachelor of Arts Degree in Psychology at the University of Puget Sound in Tacoma, Washington.

Carmela completed a Bachelors of Arts Degree in English and Spanish at Amherst College in Boston, Massachusetts.

Marc Anthony Carvajal completed a Bachelor of Science Degree at the University of Puget Sound in Tacoma, Washington and his Masters of Arts degree in Clinical Psychology at Seattle University.

Carmela, Jennifer, and Marc Anthony

We have been blessed with three adorable grandchildren; Taylor Maté, Alexander Kabacy, and Dustin Kim.

Taylor and Alexander

Dustin

PART TWO

The Way We Were

CHAPTER SEVEN

Angelitos Negros
(Little Black Angels)

    Back in 1946, every Tuesday at exactly 5 pm, mom was paid what she thought was dineralas (an enormous salary). She cleared $21.80 a week. Her pride blossomed. Before she left for work on Tuesday mornings, she invited whoever was available to meet her in front of *Kress*, when she was to get off work, to join her for the Spanish speaking Cinema.
    The lucky child would be treated to hamburgers, ice cream, popcorn and a favorite soft drink. I nominated myself to be the lucky guy. For some reason, the idea of spending three hours sitting in a theatre with mom, was not something anyone but me found acceptable. The burden to walk all the way to the department store meant sacrificing swimming time at the river, which was not something anyone else would compromise.
    Tuesday evenings were like a special date night for my mother and I. I looked forward to it all week. Finally, before I knew it, I found myself arriving in front of the department store. Mom would be waiting for me, also looking quite eager for her special evening with me. She was always pleased to see me.
    To begin our evening, Mom would hold my arm as we walked. Without a word we would walk to a nearby burger place. The attendant knew our order. Two burgers, fries and a milk shake to share, as well as one small cola. We ate silently as if it were the last meal we would

ever have. We never talked very much. She simply wanted to know how the kids were doing and I always responded that everyone was busy completing their homework and cleaning the yard. She knew I was making up a story.

The evening movies started at 5:45 on the dot. Mom would reach for the envelope she had placed tightly in her purse and would pay for two tickets. She would pay 50 cents for her ticket and 15 cents for mine. The theatre was always very dark when we entered. She cautioned me that I had to use the restroom before we sat in the dark theatre. I knew the system.

The movies were melodramas. One particular Tuesday we viewed *Angelitos Negros* (*Little Black Angels*). The week prior we had viewed previews for *Nosotros Los Pobres* (*We The Poor*). Both of these movies were very sad. I had problems unfolding the meanings and purpose of the stories.

I would always hope that the movie was going to be about Cantinflas, a funny man. No such luck. *Angelitos Negros* was about a woman that didn't like black people. That was the central theme and it bothered me a lot. On our quiet walk back home from the theatre, I spontaneously asked mom why the woman at the hacienda (villa) did not like Black people.

Instead of her usual rude response, "Callate!," she cautiously explained that the woman did not like people of color after she learned that her real mother was a woman of color. I had to take advantage of her willingness to speak to me. "Porqué mama?" ("Why, mama?"). "Ella era blanca y bonita" ("The mother was white and pretty").

Throughout the conversation, I was waiting for a negative response. She calmly responded, "No. Porque la madre de ella era mujer negra"("no, her real mother was a Black woman"). She continued, "Ella se caso con señor que era hombre blanco." ("She married a man that was White"). It was at this point that she lost me. "Ay despues vaz a comprender." ("later you will understand"). At this point I retreated while I was a bit ahead. Her explanation was totally beyond me. She seemed to respect the fact that I was already asking such questions at only eleven years old.

I later asked Maggie to explain it to me as well. She told me that the plot was about prejudice and sacrifice. It was about a woman that did not know her heritage and who was raised as the white patron's daughter. She was actually the daughter of a woman who was a black housekeeper. Maggie too, told me that I would understand later. She wondered why mom would take me to movies I could not understand.

When mom had reached for a handkerchief from her purse, I knew that it was going to be a sad movie. That night, listening intently to the story, my understanding of prejudice was subtly illustrated in the song, also named *Angelitos Negros*, which was sensitively expressed by Pedro Infante. and was originally written by Antonio Machin. Here is an excerpt:

Angelitos Negroes

"Siempre que pintas iglesias
Pintas angelitos bellos
pero nunca te acordastes
de pintar un angel negro."

Black Little Angels

"Every time, when you paint churches,
you paint beautiful angels,
but never you remembered,
to paint a black angel."

This song defined a part of the reality that was already becoming apparent to me. I was starting to understand the twisted humanity and the ugly realities of prejudice in the city across the bridge.

I was hoping that the movie we saw the past week would show again. It was a movie about a dancer by the name of Tongolele. The woman moved her hips so much I thought they would break. I liked the way she danced and danced across the screen. I asked mom if she was going to hurt her stomach? Her response was firm. "Callate, tapate los ojos" ("Shut up, cover your eyes")

I tried to hold my hand over my eyes but the music forced me to look at her hips. She was a very crazy woman, that I happened to like. When mother saw me enjoying the show, she told me that it was the last time she would ever bring me along. She didn't keep her promise.

The following week, we went to see another sad movie, *Nosotros Los Pobres*. The movie made me cry because the family was not only very poor, but each time they tried to find a way to stop being poor, something very sad happened. One good part about the movie was a very terrific singer that sang a song I remember to this day, *Amorcito Corazon* has remained in my heart throughout the years.

Five years later, I was again inspired to write poetry. This time, the intense message that the song, *Angelitos Negroes*, had engraved in my mind and in my heart, inspired me to enter a poetry competition. The event was sponsored by the *Del Río Lions Club* when I was in the seventh grade. I was guided by my cousin and teacher, Miss Teresita Rodrigues, who was also one of the best swimmers in our river. She also thought of herself as the rivers' Esther Williams- whoever that was.

To this day, I remember Teresita- not as a fearless swimmer, but as one of the most outstanding teachers who inspired my love for literature and the importance of articulating words in English. She articulated the sounds of the language without restraint. This was also the first time that I learned the difference between a vowel and a consonant. Teresita urged me not to be afraid or timid. She encouraged me to elaborate my messages as if they were the most important messages anyone had ever heard.

Four decades later I have completed an under graduate degree in English, as well as a minor in Speech and Language. I realize now that miracles do happen.

Miss Teresita Rodrigues

This is a poem I wrote, which was inspired by the original song of the same name, by Pedro Infante, so tenderly and defiantly expressed:

Little Black Angels

By Onie Carvajal

Little Black Angels you never will see.
Painted on churches or on Green Christmas trees,
You see just white angels so pure and so sweet.
But little black angels, nowhere to see
black angels away from the white
We will not forsake you in your constant fight.
I know that someday, you'll win your place in the sky.

The poem may have moved me because of the enticing voice of Pedro Infante, at the time I first heard it, or because it was my need to express the subtle racial tension that I was already experiencing in my own life. The fact that I won first prize for the poem was important to me. I received a decorated certificate and two dollars. That was my first professional award.

More significant than the award itself, was the fact that I was beginning to understand and see the struggles in which people that were not Anglo-of different skin color, like me; continued to realize that there was something different about us.

I was on a roll, so I decided to enter another writing assignment for a Lion's Club competition. It was an essay on fire prevention. A woman named Mrs. Evelyn Poag, my brother's boss, submitted the essay for me. I won another first place prize for my essay and received an additional gift certificate for $2.00.

Mrs. Poag was also one of dad's past employers and the first Anglo I had ever met. She was definitely one of those people who are not even aware they are angels. Mrs. Poag had been not just an employer, but an advocate of our family for years.

Since the days of employing my father as a painter, Mrs. Poag had hired José to work at one of her movie theatres. This one was a drive-in theatre. She later hired Raul, Francisco, and me to mow and tend to her elegant lawn. She would pick us up at the corner of our home and drive us to her amazing two-story home, where she very thoughtfully explained her expectations for the job to us. She spoke directly to me since she knew I was the foreman for the crew, which made me feel extremely important and mature. She also always encouraged me to do my best in my studies.

On the days that we worked at Mrs. Poag's house, she never let us work too long without calling us in for a snack or for lunch. One day, as she summoned me to follow her inside to her kitchen, one of her three maids interrupted her to inform her that she had a telephone call. As I waited for her return, I had a moment alone just to stand and observe her home. I scanned across the fabulous home and promised myself that someday I would have a house like hers. I would have green grass, flowers, and clean floors. I also promised myself that I would have a refrigerator with plenty of food to feed anyone who came to my house.

Just like Mrs. Poag, I insisted to myself that this would not be just another dream- it would become a reality, just like many of the wonderful things that had already happened to us. This was the beginning of my promise never to stay on the brink of failure, but to step forward to success; whatever it meant and wherever it was.

CHAPTER EIGHT

In Search of a Better Life

Several families started to move away to places like; California, Nebraska, and other parts of the United States. Lack of meaningful employment in San Felipe compelled families to find areas where they could work, save money, and eventually return to San Felipe.

When seasonal work was completed, many families returned to their barrios. Several families chose to stay in California permanently. Most relocated to areas in northern and southern California where citrus fruit and vegetable plantations were plentiful. The opportunities to earn money during the harvesting of those crops-on farms and canneries, allowed hard working families to experience financial success. Their hard work definitely paid off.

My family, perhaps, was not as eager or ready to leave home. However, we knew we had to find a way out of our difficult circumstances. Without dad or older brothers, who had already ventured out on their own, through military or personal responsibilities, we had to assess means and ways to provide for our livelihood.

My mother, Chelito, shared with us that we were broke. Aurelio Diaz, who owned the *Red and White* grocery store, could not continue extending credit to us or other families. We had to leave the area and move to California for the entire summer to look for seasonal work, so we succumbed to relocation as well. We were hoping to be able return in the fall to continue school.

For us, leaving for three months and leaving our property was not difficult. We had seen several of our neighbors leave their homes for three months. We saw our best neighbors, the Chavira family, come and go for two years in a row. We were convinced that we could leave our home and our private San Felipe creek within two weeks.

Even though the need to leave was clear, the fact that we had to leave without our dad, added a different sense of alienation. Since my dad died, nothing and no one could fill our void. We had lived five years without him and knew that someday our family had to make a strong and valiant effort to exit the barrio we had grown to love. Several other families had already left the barrio. Now, the only sentiment we had left, was the important memories and advice our dad impressed on us.

Father had tried to explain to us that our world was separated by a river known as *San Felipe Creek* that ran across both the Anglo and Mexican communities. In his tender manner, he stressed the positive aspects of our reality. He stressed that even though we were separated from the people on the other side, he earnestly hoped that the "gringitos" (an endearing name for "whites") would someday integrate with our community. He wished they would learn to accept us, allowing us to be part of their world, and they too- in ours.

My dad hoped that together, we could ultimately realize and appreciate the gifts that the river offered. He often spoke of the simple ways the river was wide in certain places, providing places to bathe, swim, fish, and even do laundry. It was even a sanctuary to some, where people could find peace and tranquility at night.

Despite the many benefits of our river, our father still cautioned us, that on some nights, when storms were approaching, the river became loud and ravaging. He firmly spoke of how the river could also be a violent killer. Dad explained to all of us that as beautiful as the river was, it could also easily take the life of a child. It could swallow us in seconds without mercy. Several times, his shocking and vivid examples, left us extremely worried for days.

Two years after our dad died, Mother Nature spontaneously proved his prophetic words as the destructive rains began.

CHAPTER NINE

The Days the Rains Came

Before we completed our plans to walk away from our home to start our journey towards California, weather started to change. In the barrio, the weather and seasons became the omens of our very lives-day to day.

The long and very hot summers in particular, gave us more than enough reasons to accept the tentativeness of our lives. The heat was always unbearable. For some reason, each early July signaled the beginning of very difficult weeks to arrive. Unmerciful heat during the late Spring and early Summers made lives intolerable.

The mood of the river was often somber, but could turn ferocious and violent within hours. Such a powerful force could change the stability of families that lived close to the river. They knew the extent of misery, that the heavy rains and muddy waters from the Río Grande, could bring them almost every year.

The first indication of trouble, was when the gray clouds moved at a fast pace during the early summer afternoons, across the skies. For some reason, horses seemed to be the first to alert the barrio that all hell would soon break loose. It was their way to warn the families that a tempestuous, dark, and angry thrashing was about to happen. Their instincts were right on the money.

Families knew that the heavy drops of rain would almost immediately turn into buckets of water that would pour down from the dark skies. The torrential water fell from the sky with a message of disaster wrapped in murderous fury. Despair, fear, and hopelessness, was felt by young and old folks who knew their lives could be swept within minutes, by the massive currents, impossible to control by useless dams and broken bridges. The warning signals were clear.

My family and nearby neighbors who lived a few feet from the river were used to the demands of the work ahead of us. Our grandfather, Don Antonio, had designed and built our home on a tall frame supported by cement blocks, ingeniously providing a degree of safety uncommon to our neighbors. This brilliant design prevented gushing currents of water from blasting through our home.

In these states of emergency, our first priority was to provide safety measures for our cats and dogs. Magdalena, my oldest sister, cleverly prepared make-shift boats, from tin pails and tubs, to accommodate space for new born puppies, kittens, and their parents. The older pets were left to fend for themselves.

The smart cats had learned to climb trees while the grown dogs learned how to scamper away to high grounds. The intensity of fear and panic was also clearly vocalized by my abuelitas' parrot Nika, who demanded to be placed on top of the roof by yelling, "Mama! Mama! Agua! Agua!" ("Mommy! Mommy! Water! Water!").

Nature reminded us time and time again, that she had power to destroy what we thought would last forever. When we finally managed to climb up to the roof of our house, we could get a clear and terrifying view of her power.

New or old, cars and houses had been swept by the forceful currents from other economically stable parts of the city of Del Río. It provided us with a lesson that nothing ever lasts, and that not even money can buy everything.

Even though the losses in our barrio were minor, it was difficult to witness the brutal outcome of the storm. The first variety of debris that passed near our house was; outhouses, tires, trash, and barrels. The second cluster were small animals such as; horses, sheep, and cows, and the third was; mattresses, furniture, and anything or anyone, that the floods had taken.

In the midst of so much devastation and tragedy, heroic and admirable evidence of the strength of the human spirit became clearly apparent. I was not a champion swimmer, but I learned that when the going gets rough, we get tougher. I saved the life of various puppies and three kittens in the same heroic way that I had rescued Nikibungeray years ago.

Three hours after the floods started to calm, my 16 year old brother Ramon heard loud screams from Señora Natividad, a lady that lived next to the river. She was ready to jump to save one of her six year old sons that had been swept into the middle of the river by the strong currents. As she attempted to jump in the river, a mud slide plopped her right into the water. She too was swept out into the water and grabbed on to a broken tree.

Like a flash of lightning, my brother Ramon dived in and grabbed the child with one arm and with the other arm he held on to the huge tree trunk that Señora Natividad was desperately clasping. The branch floated the three of them to another trunk that led them back to shore. From that moment, I told everyone who would listen, that the hero was my brother and that I had taught him how to swim.

On that day in particular, Mother Nature had shown us no mercy in return for our lack of respect. The elements of misery and hopelessness had a constant impact on the barrio people. Ironically, however, so had the elements of resiliency and hopefulness.

CHAPTER TEN

Exodus to San José

If there was ever a right time to leave San Felipe, the time was upon us. Our mother assigned a list of items we were to pack with no more than two items allowed for each of us. Everyone rushed in to pack their favorite pieces of junk. There were seven of us plus Mom.

I aptly figured, two times eight equaled a total of 16 items. We had to find space for 16 belongings in a car, that could accommodate only six people and two pieces of luggage. A second problem that we faced, was a more serious one. Our car, for some reason, only started at night. Lastly, our funds were extremely limited. We did not have enough money for gas that would take us out of Del Río, much less all the way to San José, two-thousand miles away.

Another concern, though I didn't think was serious, was that at age fifteen, I would be the main driver and Magdalena would serve as a navigator. Within moments, I started to explain to my mom the nature of our challenges. She immediately told me that my advice should be kept to myself. Period. My sister interrupted and immediately suggested that I was "right on." She was also told not to intervene. At that time I wondered why our two older brothers were not around to help us balance the voting process.

In our desperation for any semblance of a democracy, Magdalena reminded me that Ramon, the oldest, was at war defending our country and that José was now gone with his new wife to San José, where we were headed. That certainly seemed like a cloud of hopelessness.

Mom was out of sight. Thirty minutes later, she came back from our neighbor's home accompanied by an older lady, Doña Regina. Doña Regina came to us with two small boys and a cat. Somehow, mom had negotiated to provide them transportation to San José for a reasonable fare. Doña Regina would pay $25 for herself and $15 for each of her boys, totaling $55. These were one-way tickets.

Mom was arrogant enough to call everyone together. She made an officious presentation regarding the rules and regulations we had to follow. Doña Regina would be assigned to a window seat and her two grandsons would be on the floor of the front seat with Francisco, Maruca, and Payito. As a navigator, Maruca was able to use a flash light and was able to read the road map, which I could not, so she had to sit next to me. Mom, who had assigned herself the role of captain, looked sternly at me, stressing that the first person that broke the rules would have to walk back home. That was a ridiculous threat.

Doña Regina needed an explanation as to where her two pieces of luggage would fit. She also wondered how her two grandsons would fit. Immediately, mom required Francisco to leave his guitar, Payito to leave her cat, Maruca to leave her cosmetic case and curling iron, and Raul had to leave his bike. I had to leave my dog Golondrina and my tool box, which contained; two screw drivers, a pair of pliers, and a lunch box that was packed with three burritos, meant to feed the family in case of an emergency.

Everything had to go. This was the point when I had to assert myself. There had to be a level of equity. My dog Golon could not be abandoned. She had always been by my side- through many difficult years. I had also been there to support her each time she delivered a litter of puppies. I asked Maruca to be my advocate for Golondrina. She refused.

Maruca simply felt that Golon could fend for herself and her puppies. She cautioned me that when she wandered around the barrio, she would return with a new litter of puppies. The entire neighborhood knew that. She was a puppy machine. Nothing and no one could stand in her way- she would always find a way to survive and nurse her puppies.

We all knew that Golon's puppies were scattered all over the barrio. The marks on the puppies' faces were unique. One half of their face was black and brown with a hint of white and the other side was solid white.

The design was indicative of the powerful genetic markers that Golon would leave on her babies wherever she scattered them.

I had lost my case. Democracy sometimes doesn't work. Fortunately, by the time we were completely ready to depart, the day had turned to evening. It was the time when the car would bless us by starting. Within forty five miles after leaving Del Río, we got a flat tire and realized that we had no spare.

After a ten minute walk, I made it to a pay phone where I called my friend Richard. I explained to him that we had a slight snag on the way to California. We were in need of a tire to continue our journey. He was ecstatic to hear from us and wondered where in the hell we were and why he was not invited to make the trip.

Previously, Richard had told me, that he was desperate to hitch a ride with us. I assured him that now he was welcome to join us. All he needed was $40.00, a tire, tools, and no luggage. I told him that we had plenty of clothes he could rent from us. He was sold.

Within an hour, Richard found us and was embraced by mom and Doña Regina with open arms. The rest of the crew was happy to see him as well, so off we went. Richard Chapa was a God send. He was an experienced sixteen year old driver and pleasant company. Doña Regina and mother seemed to have more confidence in him than they ever had in Maruca or me.

The next flat tire happened before dark in the alps of Alpine. It was difficult to fix a tire in the mountains. Richard and I quietly walked to "borrow" a tire from a small parked truck that had been left on the road. We promised that someday our Lord would bless the owners, whoever they were. We hoped that even though we took it without permission, that as a whole family, we would be forgiven.

It took us eight days to make the three day trip to San José. Both mom and Doña Regina had experienced serious constipation and dehydration. We had to stop several times in Arizona's Death Valley. The two young boys and Payito seemed to have either slept or been passed out for most of the days we spent in the desert heat. Most of our water and crackers were gone.

As we entered Indio, California, while sleeping and driving with my eyes open, I saw a huge lake. I screamed for everyone to wake up. I quickly pulled the car over. Richard, Maruca, and I dragged everyone out of the car and threw them on the edge of the water. The kids started swimming with joy and before long every one of us started yelling with delight realizing that we had finally made it to California- completely alive.

That was all that mattered. We had finally reached our Californian Promise Land. Even though we didn't have any luggage, funds, or food, we felt happy and relieved that our blessed day had arrived. We were destined to make a whole bunch of money and to never, ever have to return to the bloody floods and awful poverty that we had known so well in our barrio.

CHAPTER ELEVEN

The Pot of Gold At Last

When we arrived in San José, we dropped off Señora Regina and her boys at one of her relatives' home, where they had been awaiting her arrival. She asked when we were planning to repay her for the $200.00 she loaned us for gas. Somehow mother would manage to reimburse her after the first paycheck we would receive from picking cherries.

Richard Chapa had already made arrangements to meet his brother who had left two years earlier. I had to call José, my older brother who had previously left our precious San Felipe to settle in California. He had married his beautiful 'football sweetheart' the day after graduation from High School. They lived in Milpitas, California- just on the outskirts of San José.

During any expedition, I was the only one allowed to contact people and I always possessed coins for payphones. Therefore, when we arrived in San José, I called Mr. Pedro Reyes. To my surprise, Joel Reyes, my friend from San Felipe, who had left the year after his graduation to get rich, answered the phone. I almost passed out from excitement. I told him that a few of us were in San José and desperately needed to reach my brother José. He demanded to know where we were. I tried to convince him that we just happened to be in the area and had to see him for a grand dinner celebration.

I called José, using the phone number I had obtained from Joel's dad. José's lovely wife, Dora, answered the phone. When she realized the person on the other end of her line was me, she cried with joy. I told her we just happened to be in the neighborhood and simply called to say hi. She invited us over for a quick snack. With the assistance of Maruca's navigation, we found their lovely place. She invited us to stay at least overnight and have a special breakfast in the morning before moving on. We would inevitably end up staying for four months.

Within five days of our arrival, by my directives, we found the famous fruit orchards. They were the same ones many of our friends gloated about each time they had returned to San Felipe with their enviable earnings. Tales of success were endless.

Our first major job attempt was at a section of San José, California which was owned by Mr. Barresa. He owned cherry orchards as far as our eyes could see. Mom assigned the role of budget officer to herself, as usual. Maruca was assigned as supervisor of a staff that included Raul and Francisco. I assigned myself the role of manager. It was difficult to identify who the workers would be. It seemed that the only working staff were Francisco and Raul.

Our six year old sister Payito, became our Mascot. During the busy hours of any given day, my siblings and I barely tolerated her needs. It was mom's responsibility to provide snacks and water whenever she needed attention.

Our typical day started at seven in the morning. We would allow enough time to have our breakfast in the car, put on our boots, and prepare to climb the enormously tall trees, which were blazing with colorful red cherries. Mr. Barresa would assign a tree to each family he hired. Our duty was to pick only the ripe fruits and allow a few days to harvest the remaining cherries.

Cherry harvesting was exciting and rewarding, but also dangerous. I assigned Francisco to gather the cherries that were clinging on the tallest branch. Raul and Maruca would harvest the cherries dangling in the middle sections of the tree. Mr. Barresa constantly reminded us that the cherries on the very top of the tree required an eighty foot ladder and also had to be picked. I cleverly retorted to Mr. Barresa that the cherries on the very top of the tree were for the birds. He didn't appreciate that, and neither did Maruca, who thought I could get us fired with my smart-aleck mouth.

My singular obligation was to empty the buckets full of cherries neatly in wooden crates and stack them in special sections under the tree we had harvested. Mom, in her meticulous ways, kept a running tab of how many boxes we had completed. During our twenty minute lunch break, she would announce to us how many more boxes we had to complete before the day ended.

We had a goal to complete at least twenty boxes a day. After each day, mother and I would announce how much money we had earned. In her disappointing tenor she would sadly announce that at ninety cents a box, we basically made only $18 in a nine hour day. After deducting $9 for lunch, gas, and other expenses, the total profit per day was less than $9.

Maruca and I had a serious talk when we returned to our car to drive back to our rented hut. In the morning, before we arrived at the orchards, we first met with Mr. Barresa and two of his staff members. We announced that we were requesting a ten cent raise for each box we completed. Instead of paying us ninety cents a crate he, would have to pay us $1.00 per crate. He flatly refused.

At noon, later that day, we flatly thanked him and left his orchards. He told us how much he admired our work but explained how he also had expenses to meet, and a family to feed. Poor guy. His explanation was crap. We understood his obligations to his family but we in turn had to be thoughtful to our needs.

With our undaunted spirits, on the way home, we stopped by a huge orchard that had signs on the road, indicating that it had need for workers. Our pathetic car was still moving as we drove to the small tent. We confidently expressed to the person in charge that we were ready to make him a lot of money, but that we were also interested in making ourselves enough money to meet our family expenses. He flatly offered us a job for a generous $1.25 per crate. With awe and excitement, we grabbed the ladders and scampered up the trees to get rich.

The car that had brought us to California was on the verge of biting the dust. Transportation was our bread and butter, as important as our water and our air. We had to have a vehicle that would take us to and from work seven days a week and also move from orchard to orchard from 6 in the morning to 7 at night.

The first day without our car, which was at the car hospital, was like sudden death. I was certain that we were finished. Joe had allowed us to borrow a car, but we still felt grim about our dilemma. We paced around in circles in our five room rental house, waiting for nothing. Fortunately, when mom was depressed she would take a very long nap. During these dreadful hours, Maruca also disappeared. I thought I had heard footsteps when she was sneaking away from the house. I honestly didn't care if she had left to go rob a bank.

I had confidence in Maruca, that she would do what was necessary. It turned out that she had gone to a loan and insurance company across the street that also sold cars. With confident demeanor she shared her urgent desperation to the manager, Mr. Wright. She shared the nature of our family's need to have an operable car in order to be able to work for the money that would cover the back payments on it, which was up to $300, or the vehicle would be repossessed. Mr. Wright summoned the owner of the business. He asked Maruca to explain her emergency to Mr. Blake. Within twenty minutes, they had reached an agreement. Maruca heroically returned to us with a $300.00 check. The loan had to be repaid in full- within three weeks.

Our drama rivaled that of a Shakespearean creation. She had explained to Mr. Wright and Mr. Blake how desperately we needed a car just to simply work the fruit orchards and make enough money to return to Texas, go back to school, and take care of our pets. I predict that the pets were a soft spot for Mr. Blake, because she had seen numerous cats roaming around his offices.

The next morning we were proud to be the only family that drove through the orchards in our green, dilapidated convertible, which was unfortunately still on its last leg.

Maruca's heroism led her to desire the new name of Maggie. Thus, Maruca was baptized as Maggie- the miracle worker. We respected her for being the most resourceful, brilliant, perceptive, and ingenious individual in the family.

Maggie remained consistent with her creative ways, throughout the following weeks in our amazing San José. In early September that year, we packed our "new," or at least now working, green convertible car that would be strictly Maggie's and mine to use and no one else's.

Unfortunately the green convertible seemed to, once again, be at the end of its rope. At least three mechanics advised us to drive the car to any used car lot on San Carlos Street, where we lived. They suggested that we quietly and swiftly trade the convertible for another vehicle that was in good health. That was an enticing recommendation.

We stopped at the car lot that had the most balloons. I commanded Raul, Frank, and Payito to buzz off- to take a walk to a close by grocery store and wait for us. They were excited to be part of the mission, even if it meant that they were not part of the negotiations.

Thirty minutes later, we found the car of our dreams. It was a black Lincoln with shiny hub caps and the rear view mirrors made it look like something a congressman in D.C. would drive during a parade. It was simply elegant, fabulous, and classy. It reminded me of a limousine.

The Lincoln Extravaganza carried a price of $900. They offered us $300 for the nearly-deceased convertible. An additional $300 was required as a cash down payment and the remaining balance of $300 would be due in two weeks. The car salesman was ecstatic. We said good riddance to the green convertible for all the pain it had caused us and thanked the salesperson for his assistance.

Moments before leaving the car lot, Maggie warned me that she was not able to unlock the trunk of our old car. I simply told her, "Chill out. That is their problem." She did not chill out and frantically responded, "No! Listen to me! I left three cases of fresh apples in the trunk. They will rot in two days!" I callously responded, "That goes to prove that it's not a perfect world."

Our newly acquired Lincoln treated us well, getting us from job to job without fuss. Within three weeks, we had enough money to repay our debts and surplus funds to take home, so we were off to pursue the final portion of our San Felipian dream.

On the way back to San Felipe, we enjoyed the second motel experience of our lives. We stopped at a small motel, that to us, seemed extravagantly equipped. It had soap, running water, clean towels, and morning coffee. We reminisced of our memories of our trip to San Antonio with our abuelito. They were sweet and vivid.

We were living the high life and never wanted to leave. We managed to convince mom that we deserved to stay at least one extra day. She immediately approved. The third day we packed our brand new shoes and colorful new clothes, preparing to make our journey back to our dear San Felipe.

CHAPTER TWELVE

It Was a Glowing and Fantastic Place

Three weeks after we returned from San José, our first priority was to purchase an electric stove for our home, an amenity that mom had always wanted. She had requested it from her Patron Saint Nuestra Señora de Guadalupe. She had answered so many prayers before; five or ten more ought to be a cinch.

Through several budget assessments, Mom and Maggie had proposed gas heaters, electrical wiring to hang ceiling lights in each room, installing windows throughout the house, as well as an inside toilet. As if an act of Congress, we gained windows and ceiling lights, though regrettably, the prayers for the inside toilet were never answered. Our budget dried up.

As if we were moving in for the first time, each one of us selected the space we would call our own. Payito and Maggie had the first pick. Frank, Raul, and I, by default, chose the living room area to be our space, which left mom to be next to the kitchen. It was more convenient for it to be accessible to her so she could begin her cooking chores for the family.

Miraculously, Golon was there to welcome us again with, not surprisingly, seven puppies. She jumped on us proudly and happily sporting her new litter. We embraced her with our love and admiration for her faithful love and devotion to us.

Golon and her puppies, along with the rest of the animals, were escorted to find their own spaces outside. It was very obvious that life had taken a turn for the best for us. We were home again. Even my dear Jackie remained loyal.

Even though we now had running water in the house, we continued to use the outdoor toilet. We still had to use the river for bathing each morning, so long as the weather was pleasant. In spite of all of that, we still had a new found appreciation for the luxuries that our life did afford us in San Felipe.

While in San José, we had been subjected to commercials that intrigued us, resulting in our use of some of the latest bath and laundry soaps. We even adopted some fabulous ways to maintain our own conditioning spa which included exercise and swimming long distances in the river. I assigned myself as the swimming coach. We were now entering an era of pride for cleanliness, hygiene, and self-care.

Self-image became an important factor in the selection of our wardrobes. After fashionably sorting through several sets of shirts, jeans, socks, shoes, and hair creams, Maggie and I selected the most splendid outfits we could find. We then gallantly walked to our kitchen to have our toast and oat meal that mom had prepared for us. This was a new routine.

Frank and Raul had been enrolled in the Escuella Amarilla. Payito was also now entering the first grade there, accompanied by her favorite lamb, Nikibungeray. Unfortunately for her, the lamb was not welcomed. It was sent home to be completely spoiled by our neighbors, who had children that played with it frequently.

When Maggie and I hopped in our black Lincoln and left for school, we slowed down to allow at least six of our neighbor friends to jump into the back seats of the car. I was the driver, so I was in charge of the music.

The responsibility of the passengers was to wave and be friendly. We hoped that our peers would wave and welcome us back. After driving down the exceptionally long Garza Street, we approached the San Felipe school. At that point, we saw a cluster of students welcoming each other for the first day of school. As we parked, over 12 students came to welcome us and admire our new *Batmobile*.

On that first day of school, we were also welcomed to many new names that had emerged from only-heaven-knows-where. It seemed that every single one of the students in the building had earned a nickname over the course of the summer. Most had been tagged by names of fish, birds, monkeys, and even insects. Either way, they were names of endearment and child's play.

My brother Francisco was nicknamed Borrado (Hazel), Payito became Lightning, Maggie was now well-known as Kika, and I went through the nicknames; Tilinges, Pepe La Peu, and Los Onis.

Students who were not nicknamed now seemed to have adopted Anglo names. Leticia became Leti, Herminia became Minnie, Luis became Butch, Cata became Kate, and so on. The students that had been away to California and other states, seemed to use English more frequently after they returned.

Other than feeling proud of wearing the new clothes I had chosen and how glad I was to see everyone, something else happened to me. A revelation hit me like a bolt of lightning. In an instant of self-awareness, I realized for the very first time, that I knew who I was destined to become. It was a weird experience, a sense that around the corner of the building, in some room somewhere, would be the crossroad that would guide me to wherever I was going.

San Felipe High School

It was that moment that enhanced my confidence, to find a meaningful place in my life that would propel me to move beyond the difficult days I had known. I knew I was entering a place that would prepare me to become the person I am today.

The building, known as San Felipe High School, was not the typical place I had known the previous two years. This time, the place glowed. It provided me with a remarkable sense that this was not simply an ordinary place anymore. It would become my second home.

A sense of certainty became apparent. A certainty that this was the place where many friendships, valuable learnings, pride, permanent and fragile relationships, and the best educators in the world, would touch my life.

CHAPTER THIRTEEN

Where Did All The Flowers Go

Past memories, especially if they were not positive, have a tendency to creep back into our minds and rule the present. This was a day when an ugly occurrence had no business ruining a perfectly happy time. It was a memory that dated back to 1952. It was four year old memory of a time when I was in the eighth grade in San Felipe.

Back then, our days were abundant with nothing but good times and aspirations to meet and embrace our youth from every angle. Our world was made of papier-mâché. The appreciation of new songs, dances, movies, and the beginnings of heart-throbs became central to our existence. Nothing else mattered.

We could go anywhere we wanted. We could break any barriers and any fences we wanted to break, simply because we were awesome. We couldn't see anything and didn't care about anything that was happening outside of our own worlds. We were cousins of Peter Pan.

On one particular Saturday, my cousin Estela and her best friend, Esmeralda; who were both in the eighth grade, stopped by the house to borrow fifty cents to attend a matinee at the Rita Theatre. As usual, because of the time it took them to get ready, they had to rush to the theatre to be on time for the double feature. Estela bought the tickets while her friend would pay for the treats.

When Estela and Esmeralda entered the theatre, they rushed to grab a seat on the main floor of the theatre. On previous visits, they had always sought seating on the upper level, where the rest of their peers would normally go.

They were quickly met by an usher and were escorted, being told that the only seats available for them were upstairs. Estela had already found several empty seats downstairs. She told Esmeralda to follow her, "Persigeme hermanita, esta muy oscuro." ("Follow me, sister, it's too dark. Take my hand.")

Within seconds, the same usher, using a flashlight, advised them that they had to find a seat upstairs. Estela, with her determined disposition told the usher that they preferred to sit downstairs. The usher immediately rushed away, apparently to fetch the manager.

Estela and Esmeralda were ready to argue. Estela wanted an explanation quickly. The manager calmly explained that all of the seats in the theaters of Texas were open to everyone. Estela was losing her cool, confused as to why there seemed to be a problem. She firmly responded, "So what?" The usher added, "The law requires that the main floor is available only for Whites." The guy was nervously uttering half of his sentence when Estela told Esmeralda, "Let's get the hell out of here before I beat the hell out of this idiota." Esmeralda took Estela's arm and said, "Vamonos hermanita, vamonos." ("Let's get outa her sister.")

On their way home that day, Estela and Esmeralda walked along, totally dumbfounded with a deep sense of humiliation and confusion. It seemed that their young lives that had previously been wrapped up in a sense of positive self- esteem, was suddenly threatened by the taint of the great American lie. Betrayal of any form- for any reason, is essentially unforgivable. It is also not forgotten. Their respect and appreciation for the freedom our forefathers had proclaimed so sincerely, turned out to be fake- right before their very eyes on a Saturday afternoon.

For the rest of her high school years, my precious Estela and I, talked about the incident and walked forward with caution. We had reached a point of realization that the world outside was not always a kind one. Beyond that, we never understood exactly what had happened or why. Something had to change in our environment to stop the offensive segregation that caused us to feel inferior and vulnerable.

Unfortunately, segregation didn't stop. It only got worse. Maruca and my cousins, who were all four years older than I, remember very well that for some reason, even the swimming pools were off limits. I eventually learned that the areas of the river we felt so proud of, where my Mexican friends and I swam, became derogatorily known as the "Pig Pen."

Any and all public facilities, were off limits to people of color. Apparently we were people of color too. It became clear that not everyone had the rights and privileges we thought we had.

Even World War II Veterans, who were not white, were not allowed to enter facilities such as; restaurants, barber shops, swimming pools, and other public places. The numerous signs that read, "Non-Whites Allowed" became the standard of justice in our precious Del Río.

We had been raised believing a lie. This was not what our teachers had told us in our elementary schools. Evidently, they did not tell us the complete truth. We were told that America was a land of the brave and the free; a land that God himself had blessed for all Americans.

We were taught to pledge our allegiance to the flag of the United States of America. We were sometimes even inspired to sacrifice our lives to be keep our country free from our enemies. We suddenly realized that there were enemies among us. We had even been taught that Washington could not tell a lie.

It became clearly ironic that our brothers, uncles, and friends, who had sacrificed their lives for the freedom of all U.S. citizens, apparently did not earn the freedom to be part of any place in America, for a stupid reason such as skin color.

Instead of accepting them with applause and pride for their bravery and commitment to their country, they came home to be victims of segregation, prejudice, derogation, and inhumane rejection. They came to read blatant signs that indicated that no Mexicans were allowed and that the establishments were open for "Whites Only".

"Pintor, si pintas con amor
Porque despracias tu color
Si sabes que en el cielo
tambien los quiere Dios".

CHAPTER FOURTEEN

A Difficult Transition

After the glitter and gentry of our days had subsided, our family once more encountered the need to examine our finances. Our much admired and appreciated electric stove was on a list for repossession. One of Joe's friends worked as a pick up boy for such items, items in default of nonpayment.

Nieves Flores was the kindest and most thoughtful individual. He showed up one day with his boss, but first tried explaining to mom that he had orders to repossess the stove. He didn't know the hell they were about to face. Mom would not allow them to enter the kitchen. Instead, she took the hose, opened the faucet to full blast, and armed with three pots, went after both of them with a fury the poor guys had never known.

When Joe came home, we all ran to him and urgently explained why mom was so angry. Prieto, as he had become known, had a natural tendency of always looking for a fight. Having a perfectly good reason for battle, he bolted out the door and went to confront Nieves and his boss.

We never knew what happened. Whatever it was, we were grateful to be able to keep the stove, arrange smaller payments, and never had to hear from the company again. This embarrassing experience gave mom the platform she had been waiting for to talk to us.

Mother insisted that Prieto and I, would find part time jobs. Before long, both of us were fortunate to find jobs at the two drive-in theatres.

Mom insisted that Prieto would be my mentor and job supervisor after school was dismissed.

My job was simple. All I had to do was gather the trash left by customers, that had attended evening movies, at both the *Ceniza* and the *Gay Ninety* drive-in theaters. The jobs gave us ample time to attend school from 8 am to 3:30 pm, though we had to rush to work from 4 to 6 pm and return home to get our homework done, while preparing for the next day of school.

In theory, our plans were ambitious, but in reality, implementing those plans was lousy. I could not find the time I needed to get everything accomplished. Ironically, Prieto was creative enough to find time for football. Perhaps it had something to do with the fact that he had the car.

I continued to face the demands of part time work at both theatres. To ease my tensions, I hired my brothers, Frank and Raul, to help me with some tasks. As days went by, someone reported us to our supervisor, Mrs. Poag, by telling her that she was in violation of child labor laws. Responding to the concerns of the "Nosey Roseys"- as she referred to the snitches, Mrs. Poag was obligated to release Frank and Raul. Prieto continued serving as manager of the concession stand in the evenings.

I continued doing minimal maintenance tasks, though I was not allowed to work in the concession stand. Mrs. Poag was generous enough to allow me to continue to work, if only to pick up trash after school. Prieto, at this time, remained in charge of my duties.

On the side, Prieto became a superb, admired, and gallant *Mustang* running back football star. My glory was the opportunity of finding loose change and items of abandoned clothing found at the drive inns. I was able to sell the items at a yard sale with Maggie's help on certain weekends. We had found another way to get rich again.

I didn't have a social or an academic life. While in school I slept with my eyes wide open. After completing my home chores, demanded from Mom, I would return to work to gather trash- getting the theater grounds ready for the evening movies and customers. Eager to get my foot into concessions, I was even starting to learn the steps needed to make popcorn. Somehow I was forgiven for the assumed violation of working as a child.

Weekends were my best days. Prieto was a good supervisor. He started to teach me the responsibilities involved in concession work. He expected that someday I would be old enough to take over his duties when he would inevitably graduate from High School. This could be an amazing opportunity for me.

I dreamed of eating popcorn and hotdogs smothered with Chile, to my heart's content- for the rest of my life. I could also drink and feast on ice cream sundaes whenever I wanted to. I even became obsessed with the idea of someday being selected to play a significant part in a movie, or at least have a theater of my own. I simply had to learn the tricks of the trade from my brother.

Before I got carried away with my grandiose thinking, I snapped back into reality, realizing that I had to get back to the concession stand and assist my brother with the early customers. As I started walking towards the concession stand, I saw a black cat with a white stripe on its tail, staring at me, with a vicious look. The damn cat lifted its tail, aiming directly at me. It was a damn skunk.

The merciless skunk sprayed me, producing the most horrific odor I had ever smelled. Along with the odor, there was also a burning sensation on my chest, which filled me with fear. Not realizing the magnitude of the odor, I ran to find my brother.

When I arrived at the concession stand, people were already lined up, ready to order their snacks. As soon as I walked inside, they scampered out as fast as their feet would take them. Immediately, my brother pushed me out and told me to stay clear away, remove my white overalls outside, and walk home.

As soon as I arrived at home, mom and my siblings quickly told me to get out and to go jump in the river. I was told not to get out of the water until my brother Prieto returned. I felt safe because I knew that no snakes or water turtles would come near me.

The following day, I was the talk of the town- the smell of the school. That was the day Arturo and his buddies baptized me as Pepe Le Pue, a French cartoon skunk. Arturo and his sick buddies walked behind me down the hall chanting as they emulated a French accent; "Do not come with me to the casbah. We shall make beautiful musin' togezzin' right here." It was so stupid.

I continued my high school days like a Zombie. It was easy to dream and pretend of my existence in theater life. Going through the motions of surviving as a student in each classroom, in front of teachers, was another matter. I was called on the carpet many times by every single one of my stringent and caring teachers. They shared a list of concerns; I had been late to class at least three times, had not been submitting assignments when due, or I would leave class before the bell rang.

Mother was invited to be present for a final conference. After that session she required me to share my daily attendance, assignments, and grades on each assignment with the original signatures from my teachers. I wondered why she required original signatures. I felt like I had been sentenced to Alcatraz. Even that sounded more humane than this.

Beyond monitoring, she requested how I would change my work schedule to meet my teachers' homework assignments and attendance. She gave me an ultimatum: either improve school performance or abandon employment at the drive-in. That was final. This was the first time I knew mom did not realize that I had only two arms. I felt trapped with high expectations.

During those days, cell phones had not yet been invented. Strangely, however, if and when I missed completing and submitting homework assignments or missed a class, mom would find out within minutes. The threat of having flying-monkey-spies monitoring my life was haunting. I had to comply. There was no way out.

CHAPTER FIFTEEN

A Dual Personality

During one of my exhausting afternoons, I dragged myself to my biology class with Mr. Gutierrez, who was a favorite teacher. That afternoon, I discovered an important truth about my learning habits. As usual, I actually took notes or drew whatever designs or illustrations he had prepared for his lectures. He was extremely well organized and easy to understand. Listening to him inspired me to someday be a scientist.

Mr. Gutierrez had a colorful print entitled *The Human Brain*. He made the mistake of informing us that most, if not all mammals, had a brain that looked something like the illustration he displayed for us. He supported his illustration by saying, "Don't worry if and when, your parents share with you, a menu that offers barbequed cessos. Cow cessos are special menu items in the Mexican culture. They are very nutritious and good for you."

The first time I had ever heard or seen the term "brain," was when my Abuelito had bought delicious barbecue he called "cessos." We ate the very soft and delicious meat with beans and hot salsa he had prepared himself.

Mr. Gutierrez continued, "The purpose of today's lecture is to illustrate to you that the human brain is more complex and complicated than the brains of cows, sheep, and monkeys. Even though some monkey's brains are well advanced, our brains are way ahead of them." He continued, "Enough of that. Those of you who take an advanced class in human anatomy will learn more about the human brain and other parts of our anatomy."

Gutierrez continued his lecture, pointing to the colorful illustration of the human brain on the blackboard. When he spoke, he looked at me, warning me to remember the important terms he had labeled on the brain. He seemed to know that mom had placed me on probation and that I had to do well in every class. He also cautioned us that we would have a quiz the following day on the Brain lecture. He stressed that the quiz would be worth 35 points.

Speaking emphatically, Mr. Gutierrez said, "The human brain is divided into two major sections; the right brain and the left brain. Each side of the brain has specific functions. The right side of the brain is best at expressive and creative tasks, such as; music, expressing and reading emotions, colors, and intuition…" At that point I raised my hand and told him that the word intuition confused me. He seemed pleased that I asked. He explained, "Intuition is the ability to know and understand ideas by quick insight, by hunch, and just by knowing. I call intuition the 'Aha!' of life. Many gifted people are intuitive. They simply know, by sensing what the right solution to problems are, on their own."

I was somehow disappointed. My teacher's response certainly didn't help. I thought the 'aha' word was silly. He continued, "The left brain is better in helping us with numbers, critical thinking, logic, language, and reasoning." He went on to explain that right-brain people were more thoughtful and subjective and that left-brain folks were more analytic and objective.

As if intuitively, I immediately knew that I was right-brain dominant and no one would ever change that. I had always felt that I walked lop-sided with my head always leaning to the right. By the end of the hour, he explained that the right and left hemispheres of the brain were separated by a structure known as the Corpus Coliseum. By that time I was doomed. I even forgot to study for the quiz the next day.

The next day, I sleep walked to Mrs. Marie Kellers' Algebra class. I thought my brain would never allow me to be interested in the symbols she wrote on the board nor the reason why the symbols were important. The worse reality is that Mrs. Keller knew that I had zero interest in anything she presented.

Mrs. Keller had tried, in every way possible, to rediscover and re-experience the gifted ability my brother Ramon had demonstrated in her class six years earlier. In spite of her thoughtful and generous approach to teaching, nothing seemed to work for me.

On occasion, we were assigned to work in groups of three. Fortunately, Mrs. Keller assigned me to be with Joe Gonzalez and Arturo Cuellar in a group. They were the wizards in analytical thinking and logic- totally left-brain guys. They could dissect algebra problems in minutes while I worried if I had ordered enough hot dogs and buns for the evening customers at the theater. We lived and functioned in two different worlds.

Mrs. Keller

One afternoon, Mrs. Keller assigned an algebra problem to us, asking me to work out the problem on the board. She required me to show, step-by-step, how I would find the solution. At that very moment, I felt my death was imminent.

My legs would not allow me to walk. My hands went numb, and sweat, dripping from my brow, blurred my vision. Heroically, Arturo and Joe Gonzales intervened, temporarily saving me by explaining to Mrs. Keller that I was scared of speaking in front of people. It was a blatant lie.

Mrs. Keller must have seen through my avoidance and therefore, would not back off. She insisted that the following day I had to comply with the assignment. When the bell rang I still couldn't move. Art spoke to me, "Los Onis, you have an attitude problem. You have been telling yourself that you hate math with a passion and you believe it. You are one of the smartest friends I have."

Arturo gave me some advice, saying "Let's talk to Mrs. Keller and see if she can allow you to take the class next semester when you are ready." He continued, "Tell her you have many hot dogs on your plate."

Taking heed in Arturo's wisdom, I confronted Mrs. Keller. When I did, she gave me a huge smile and embraced me. I told her I would be working on my left-brain. Hearing me say that, Arturo added, "My friend, don't believe that nonsense."

The Spring semester of the ninth grade nourished my right brain. Mrs. Pasley had proven the left-brain-right-brain theory in my eyes. This semester would be the semester of my doom or the time to shine if there was any shine left.

There was an emphasis on American Literature. Our task was to read American poetry, essays, and novels written during the Romantic period. We read poems written by Keats, Browning, Longfellow, and plenty of others. We read essays by Ralph Waldo Emerson and Robert Frost, to name a couple.

This was the semester when my total brain revived. I read during mornings, afternoons, and evenings before and after work. I would stay in the classroom long after class was dismissed and read until it was time to take Romelia to work, all the way across town, where she worked as a clerical assistant for an attorney.

I would talk to Romelia about the literature we had been reading and the very important messages they presented. She agreed saying, "The entire class is burning with interest." She, herself, was nailed to Elizabeth Barrett Browning's poem, *How Do I Love Thee*.

Arturo was reading a poem by Robert Frost, *The Road Less Traveled*, and Mary Treviño was fascinated by Emily Dickenson's poetry. I spent most of my time in the library or at home, reading essays by Ralph Waldo Emerson.

Mrs. Pasley was one of the most brilliant and creative teachers. We were fortunate to have her during that semester. She challenged us to select a passage of literature from any writer and present excerpts of the writing at an afternoon assembly. We would be required to present a three minute oratory.

I had been reading Emerson's essay on nature. Within the essay, Emerson divided nature into four usages; commodity- how we use nature in our lives, beauty, language, and discipline. I had been reading the stage on discipline for days. I selected one of his essays entitled, *Self-Reliance that Addresses the Concept of Discipline.*

In preparation for the oratory, I had practiced for three days and even had Maggie time my presentation. When it was time for me to get on stage in front of all my friends and many teachers, I looked around the auditorium and started reading the lines I had selected. I felt a surge of confidence that I had never experienced before.

I spoke slowly, "I have selected an Essay from one of my most favorite writers of the Romantic Period. His name is Ralph Waldo Emerson who wrote an essay on nature. In his essay he separated four parts of nature; commodity, beauty, language, and discipline."

I read aloud, parts of his essay entitled, *Self Reliance*, where he addresses the idea of self-discipline;

"What I must do is all that concerns me, not what the people think. This rule equally arduous in actual and intellectual life, may serve for the whole distinction between greatness and meanness. It is the harder because you will always find those who think they know what is your duty better than you know it. It is easy in the world to live after the worlds' opinion, it is easy in solitude to live after our own; but the great man is he who in the midst of the crowd, keeps with perfect sweetness the independence of solitude. A political victory, a rise of rents, the recovery of your sick, or the return of your absent friend, or some other favorable event, raises your spirits, and you think good days are preparing for you. Do not believe it. Nothing can bring you peace but yourself. Nothing can bring you peace but the triumph of principles."

When I finished reading, I slowly walked down the stairs to sustained applause.

The following day, I experienced a subconscious fear I had about my job. I was afraid that my brother, Prieto, was going to make me take over his job at the concession stand. I was suspicious because he was walking me through every single detail of the job. No one ever asked me, or warned me, that this was on somebody's agenda. That evening I had a dream of skunks and hot dogs.

My fear was quickly becoming reality. It was at this point, that I came apart. Prieto outlined, step-by-step, the horrors I would experience. He slyly boosted me, speaking of the good qualities I had. I was confident, worked hard, and was very likeable. I wanted him to say more, but that was it.

Prieto gifted me with a list of negatives as well, going on to say that I had too many friends, "Get rid of them. Don't give out anything for free. No passes. No free popcorn. No free drinks." He bluntly stated that those rules applied to Maggie and her friends as well.

He continued, "Not for Pulga, Joel, Chapa, tu prima(your Cousin) Estela, or girlfriends. Get rid of them." I kept nodding with affirmation.

During his speech I crossed my fingers. There was no way I could ever give up my friends. Not for all the tea or hot dogs in China. Just listening to Prieto was the toughest part of his lesson. He spoke in a stern voice, sounding like Father Santos, when my family and I were excommunicated from the Catholic Church.

My brother softened his tone to deliver the remainder of his speech. I felt like he was reading my last rites:

"You are responsible to order everything that is needed to run the Concession Stand. Do you hear? Everything. You will be accountable for everything the very day it's delivered. You will be responsible for every sale you make every evening. One by one; popcorn, candy, drinks, ice cream, hot dogs, and everything else. Each evening, at closing, you will be required to make a detailed inventory of what was sold, clear the cash Register, and place every cent that customers paid, in the bag under the cash register."

I was looking forward to my last meal before execution as Prieto's speech continued, "You will also be responsible to require the person in charge of the ticket gate to give you a receipt of each admission ticket she sells. When you collect the money at the end of the evening, you will have to be sure that each dollar, each nickel, each dime, each cent, matches the number of tickets that have been sold. You cannot go home until this is done."

Prieto cautioned me, "After you collect the funds and receipts, you have to take the money bags from the concession stand and gate admissions downtown to the Rita Theatre." The drive in theater was nearly three miles away- a long way for me to carry money after dark.

I asked, "How am I supposed to get from here to downtown without a car?" Prieto responded, "A security guard will pick you up here and drive you to the theater. Then he will walk you to the safe. You open the combination locks, place the bags inside, shut the metal door, and twist the combination. After that, you have to walk home by yourself."

By the time Prieto finished listing my new responsibilities, I was trembling. When I stepped out of the concession room, my left brain, if I had one, went completely dormant. I excused myself to vomit. Maggie was sitting in the car waiting for me. I told her my brother was crazy. She agreed.

CHAPTER SIXTEEN

Miracle of Miracles

The same week I was named the official concession stand Manager, I celebrated my 18th birthday. The word got out. I had the keys to the concession. Walking down the hall, many of my friends reached out to congratulate me on my promotion. During classes, several teachers earnestly conveyed to other students, how my hard work rewarded me with earned success.

I walked through the halls, feeling quite modest about the praise I had been receiving from everyone. I knew full-well, that proving my capability, would be the next critical step. I had to prove to myself and mom, that I could be successful at work, while still finding time to meet the expectations from teachers in each of my classes.

It was the second half of my Junior year. For some reason, I felt more confident and stable than I had felt for a long time. I truly felt that I could handle the responsibilities of the job and schedule time to complete class assignments as well. Mom gave me the freedom: to do or to die.

There were two positive factors guiding me. Primarily, I knew that I had the support of my outstanding teachers. Every single one, without exception, were quality educators. I had been told numerous times that if a student would encounter **one** outstanding and caring teacher through the years in school, that they should consider themselves lucky.

I was blessed to have twelve out of twelve teachers that were simply superior. Even if I didn't quite perform to my absolute best, they were there to devote time to me. The same they did with other students, to help everyone do the best that they could. I felt valued.

The other positive factor was the realization that we had to have both sides of our brain working in balance to accomplish the many intricate tasks in our lives. My new experience in crunching numbers derived from the practical application of math on the job, which occurred on a nightly basis. I was also appreciating the powerful sentiments in poetry, suddenly making it clear that I could advance in more than one area. For a change, I felt intelligent.

For some reason, my two brains, after negotiating with each other, allowed me to meet the demands of my new life. In fact, not only did my logical and analytical capabilities evolve, but my social life also blossomed- to no end.

To make life more amazing, that same year I developed a beautiful and special relationship with Romelia Guardia. Simply knowing her, added a very important element to my life I had never experienced before. Yep, love was a many splendored thing.

CHAPTER SEVENTEEN

Precious Slices of Life

  With the two hemispheres of my brain finally working together, each day as soon as I reached the long and shiny hallway of my school, work preoccupations faded away. I was able to embrace the positive aspects of my life as soon as I entered the rooms where I encountered the graceful appreciation of my great friends and teachers, once more.

  An hour after I had arrived one day, walking towards Mrs. Pasley's class, I immediately took my usual front seat by the window. It seemed that everyone in class had a tendency of occupying the same seats they had chosen on day one. When Mrs. Pasley walked in with her radiant smile, satchel in hand, she would call on each of us for attendance, greeting us with a genuine expression of "good morning."

  Viewing the sky and feeling the soft breeze, enhanced a sense of thankfulness for being part of this special place and surrounded by so many of my friends. The fresh air energized me, preparing me for Mrs. Pasley's meaningful lectures. That morning, her lecture was on the topic of poetry most of us had found difficult to understand.

Mrs. Pasley

One day before her lecture, she thoughtfully asked Nelda Laing to share with us, her favorite song. Nelda was stunned. She frantically responded, "I have many favorites. I guess I have a lot of favorites." Mrs. Pasley encouraged her, "Well any song from last year or this year, from any movie..." Nelda interrupted, "I guess the song by Nat King Cole, *Pretend*."

After Nelda had broken the ice, Diamantina Peralez, as usual, eagerly raised her hand and blurted out "I like the song by Patsy Cline, *Crazy*." The class laughed. Mrs. Pasley responded, "that is a very popular song by a well-known singer and artist." Subsequently, three other hands went up. Mrs. Pasley reacted, "Okay, okay, so this is your assignment for tomorrow..." She requested, "write the title of your favorite song, underline the title, and explain in half a page why this song is your favorite." As what had become usual for Mrs. Pasley, she stressed, "Write in your Sunday penmanship. I'll return your homework assignment to you within two days."

After Mrs. Pasley delegated her assignments, she continued her lecture. She gave each of us a copy of a poem that she had duplicated for us. On top of the page, the title read: *ODE: Intimations of Immortality from Recollections of Early Childhood.* To me, the title was very long and very difficult to understand. It simply turned me off. I was certain that this was going to be boring.

I started looking out the window, wishing that I was swimming in my river instead. I always used to wish that I could be half fish. Every time that the hum-drum day-to-day didn't make sense, if I was close to my river, I would plunge right in.

Day dreaming, I was so far away in my mind I could barely hear Mrs. Pasley's voice, "Antonio, on top of the page there is a title. Please read it for us." I snapped back to reality and answered her request, "ode…and something else…" I paused, "I don't know how to read those words."

Mrs. Pasley thoughtfully replied, "I am sure you don't. You see the word 'ode' comes from three different periods in literature. It comes from Latin, French, and Greek literature." She emphasized, "It comes from many, many years back."

Mrs. Pasley explained to us that the word *ode*, meant song. She continued, "You see, each of you just wrote the name of an ode- a song. An ode is a poem marked by an exaltation of feelings. It also means that the song is very long. The numbers you see on the right hand margin are the number of lines in this poem. This poem is one hundred and fifty lines long. You see, the songs you like, are poems set to music. Can someone sing the song they chose for us?"

Diamantina, my very special friend, without being called on or even raising her hand, sang out in an emotional tempo, "Crazy, I'm crazy for feeling so lonely."

Diamantina was wrapped up in her message. She continued her song.

Almost in tears and blushing, Diamantina suddenly stopped. The class applauded. The students who were sitting near her stood up and hugged her while applauding her so loudly Mrs. Pasley had to ask us to settle down.

Diamantina, with artistic charm, stood up and bowed to us. The applause continued. Even our serious, though elegant teacher, gave in and applauded her. "Phew!" Mrs. Pasley proclaimed, "We have a star that has been born before our very eyes today."

Mrs. Pasley suddenly shifted back to her lecture, telling us that she wanted us to be thinking of future homework assignments that would be inspired by our readings. She continued, "The next word in the title is 'intimations.' This is probably a new word for some of you."

I was spontaneously called on, "Antonio, what does the word mean to you?" I was totally caught by surprise, still thinking about the song *Crazy*. Quickly shifting gears, I confidently answered, "It means to be able to know by just knowing. It's something that you already know. It means *aha*."

Hearing my response to Mrs. Pasley's question, the class seemed puzzled and silent. Mrs. Pasley interjected, "The word you are defining so well means *Intuition*." She wrote the word on the board along with the word, *Intimation*. The words looked and almost sounded the same to me. I then realized that similar sounding words can carry very different meanings.

Even though I was incorrect with the definition I supplied, Mrs. Pasley told me, "I am proud that you are trying." She digressed, "The word intimations means a subtle hint." As if she were a spelling bee moderator, I asked her to use the word in a sentence. She was elated that I had asked. She replied, "Antonio, you are intimating to me that you appreciate literature. I take the hint."

The class solidly connected after Mrs. Pasley's clever response. This was indeed a teachable moment. She went on, "Well, now that we have sparks flying all over the room, let's try the next word in the title." Searching for her next volunteer, she called on Mary, "Miss Treviño, what does the word immortality mean to you?"

Mary had a lot of my respect, and in my biased opinion, was also one of the most charming and intelligent girls in the class. She didn't know what the word meant but made an admirable effort anyway. Speaking softly she uttered, "I think the word comes from the word mortal. Something that does not live forever…like us, we are mortals. That's all I know."

"Excellent effort!" Mrs. Pasley praised. She explained that the word *mortal* means something that does not live forever. She briefly lectured, "The prefix, 'im' in 'immortal' means something that does live forever. It is something that is unending. It has no end. It never dies."

Molly Cardenas asked if a memory or a song can live forever. Mrs. Pasley gasped. She complimented her, saying, "Wow! Molly, you are way ahead of me already. Good for you." She selected another student, "So now Henry, would you please read the entire title?" Henry read aloud, "Intimations of Immortality From Recollections of Early Childhood."

Mrs. Pasley called on Nani next, "So what does the entire title mean?" Nani, in her determined self-confidence responded, "It means that there is a hint that memories of our childhood can be unending-that memories can last forever as long as we can remember them." Mrs. Pasley was obviously overwhelmed with appreciation for such a brilliant response.

Nani proceeded to ask, "Who was Mr. Wordsworth?" Mrs. Pasley excitedly replied, "Excellent question. He is a famous author who wrote many poems and sonnets about nature." She expanded, "If you read each line thoughtfully, he writes about his appreciation for nature after his mother died when he was eight years old."

The thought of Mr. Wordsworth losing his mother at the age of eight, made me extremely sad, forcing me to recall the loss of my own father. Mrs. Pasley wrapped up the hour. She announced, "Tomorrow, we will continue by reading the first stanza from his ode. I already know that most of you will make excellent future teachers. I have learned so much from you."

CHAPTER EIGHTEEN

Superman Drops His Cape

After such an unusually perfect day in school, that evening, my work at the drive-in was also productive. I had reflected seriously on the nature of my job. It was impossible to complete the requirements of the job single handedly. The duties required a team- a coalition. I asked Mrs. Poag if I could hire Maggie to be my assistant. Mrs. Poag's trust in my judgment, landed me a new employee.

I felt that Maggie would be especially useful in the hot dog department. Aside from ordering whatever was needed to serve hot dogs, she could also take full responsibility to prepare and serve them. Mrs. Poag had always been impressed by Maggie's charm and pleasant personality. Her people skills were badly needed as well, and now, we would have them. I also trusted Maggie to monitor the area where most of the food was served, so I added serving popcorn to her list of responsibilities.

My brother Prieto, had abandoned me to adopt his managerial duties. He was later convinced by Mrs. Poag to work at least half-time, in the projection room- to run the films. I realized I also had a need to identify and recruit another person for the beverage counter. This person would be responsible for serving cold or hot drinks and water when necessary. Without a doubt, it was the hardest area to keep clean. I asked Mrs. Poag if I could also add my cousin, Estela, to the crew. She approved. Now we were a family drifting on the same boat going to only-heaven-knows-where.

The next day, in a fully attended class room, there was standing room only. I had arrived fifteen minutes early, thus securing myself a seat. By 9:05, or twenty minutes thereafter, every seat in the room was taken. While we waited for Mrs. Pasley to arrive, a loud chattering murmur resounded through the room.

While we waited, I was fascinated to hear the rumors of couples going steady, breaking up, or being selected for sports and musical activities. I also heard of students competing for special recognition to be featured in a book called *El Conquistador*. It sounded important. I started to become aware of another part of our school environment I had not seen before.

I was fascinated to hear about all of the things that my peers were taking part in. They participated in many social activities that were part of the school. Because my daily schedule took me to another focus after school, where I had to prepare for my evening job, this social aspect was foreign to me.

My schedule required me to be at work by 4pm. I had to prepare whatever food there was that had to be warmed up, getting it ready to serve at the exact time when the ticket box office opened for business. I felt like I had no social life whatsoever. I pretty much didn't.

When Mrs. Pasley finally came in, the room quieted down quickly. She continued the content of the lecture, exactly where she had left off the day before. She encouraged questions. Abigail opened with, "What is a stanza?" Mrs. Pasley answered, "It's a group of words in the poem. It's the division of words as you see in this poem. It consists of a series of lines arranged together. Diamantina gave us an excellent example of how, the emotional song she sang so well, was grouped into lines."

Mrs. Pasley stayed on point and spoke, "So let's start reading the second stanza of the poem. Romelia, will you please read?" Romelia read aloud with a sweet voice:

"There was a time when meadow, grove, and stream…
The earth, and every common sight to me
did seem appareled in celestial light,

The glory and the freshness of a dream...
It is not now as it hath been of yore; Turn wheresoe'er I may
By night or day,
The things which I have seen I now can see no more."

Romelia was exhilarated by, in what a beautiful way, the message was written. Mrs. Pasley, in her usual affirmation, agreed and spoke, "You see how powerful the poet presents the imagery. I can see the landscape so vividly." She paraphrased, emphasizing on portions of the piece, "There was a time when meadow, grove, and stream...the earth did seem appareled in celestial light...The things which I have seen I now can see no more."

Mrs. Pasley questioned us, "Well, what is the message? It is probably difficult for you to understand." She told us that the poem was written in old English and was from the year of 1850. That was more than a hundred years ago.

Impressed with the antiquity of the poem, Teno exclaimed, "Wow! That is a longtime. No wonder I can't understand it." Nodding her head, Mrs. Pasley added, "Well, poetry is difficult to understand because the poet has his or her own ideas at what the lyrics meant to them when they wrote it. Each stanza has a message."

Mrs. Pasley soon clarified the purpose of reviewing such ancient literature. She explained to us, "It is up to us to interpret what we think the words mean to us today." Moving forward into an interactive activity, she made a request, "I would like you to split into groups of four and discuss what the stanza means to you. After your discussion I want you to identify a leader in your group that will share with us what your group decides."

We were given ten minutes to discuss and interpret the meanings of the stanza. Each group was then given three minutes to share with the class. Three groups had found similar commonalities in within the first five lines. Four other groups shared similar interpretations of the last four lines.

Mrs. Pasley appreciated each, though slightly different, interpretation of the lines that were presented. She stated, "It's important for us to know the purpose of this poet's message. As I mentioned earlier, his mother died when he was eight years old." Then she added, "Sadly, William Wordsworth's father also died when he was in grammar school. He and his four other brothers and sisters were left orphans."

Hearing about the loss of William's parents and the sadness of orphaning, it was that very moment, that my heart wept for him. I felt tears streaming down from my eyes. It was difficult to even breathe. Mrs. Pasley sought her next presentation and asked, "Mary, will you please read the third stanza?" Mary was eager to share:

"The Rainbow comes and goes,
And lovely is the rose…but yet I know, wher'er I go
That there hath passed away a glory from the earth."

Mrs. Pasley tenderly continued selecting volunteers, "Mr. Linian, will you read line 60?" Joe Linian thoughtfully read aloud:

"Our birth is but a sleep and a forgetting
The soul that rises with us, our Life's Star,
Hath had else where it's setting
And cometh from afar
Not in entire forgetfulness,
And not in utter nakedness,
But trailing clouds of glory do we come
From God, who is our home."

Touched, Mrs. Pasley expressed, "Joe, you read the stanza very eloquently." At this point Mrs. Pasley chose lines she thought were significant and then asked me to read the last stanza. I gladly accepted the part. I read out loud:

"Though nothing can bring back the hour,
Of splendor of the grass, of glory in the flower,
We will grieve not, rather find
Strength in what remains behind."

After I read, I felt the sensation of sadness, choking me up again. Mrs. Pasley softly intervened and asked us to concentrate on the last lines: She tenderly read:

"Thanks to the human heart by which we live,
Thanks to its tenderness, it's joys, and fears.
To me, the meanest flower that blows can give
Thoughts that do often lie too deep for tears."

Mrs. Pasley concluded, "Class, I have read this poem many times before. However, your sensitive interpretations have evoked my tears. This is the first time this poem has meant so much to me." She went on to say, "Now that you have been acquainted with some of the most respected and appreciated excerpts, written by such a sophisticated and gifted English poet, your assignment due next week should be more meaningful to complete. Your task is to write a one page narrative of your favorite childhood memory." Not surprisingly, she finished by saying, "Remember, Sunday penmanship is required."

CHAPTER NINETEEN

A Three Ring Circus

My evenings at the drive-in allowed me to shift gears and appreciate a different reality. Challenges were unpredictable. Maggie and my cousin Estela provided me with an excellent sense of support for both, major and minor, unexpected scenarios that we could encounter, minute-to-minute, each evening that we opened the doors for business.

The door next to the cashier's desk was used as an exit and the entrance door was by the popcorn stand. Surely, such a system was a clever profit-driving ruse that was designed with intent. Customers would order their popcorn, hot dogs, and chips when they entered the south door, swiftly moving forward for their drinks and ice cream.

Since I had assigned myself the role of cashier, I was also responsible for the sale of candy bars and gum. Maggie and Estela were confident at their stations. I however, was a clumsy cashier and candy salesman, mainly because of my multiple roles of; collecting money, giving exact change on the spot, and being responsible to lean forward to reach for candy from the case.

Mrs. Poag usually stopped by to get chocolate mint candy for dessert. I always suspected that she was actually there to evaluate our three ring circus performance. After three weeks of our show, she asked me how I thought I could rearrange our responsibilities. I immediately, suggested that we should hire a cashier to help me with my overwhelming responsibilities. I needed to be free from monitoring ticket sales at the front gate, at the end of the evening, to be able to prepare the report for concession earnings.

Given the opportunity to speak freely, I also suggested that I should be free to move around from each serving space to be able to help Maggie and Estela with the sudden crowds that came in during the fifteen minute intermission. Mrs. Poag, in her remarkably respectful approach, as was her role as owner of the theatres in Del Río, had an amazing philosophy of allowing the staff to assess their own responsibilities.

I learned considerably about my strengths and weaknesses as a concession manager. Interestingly, I also learned to appreciate my aptitudes in dealing with an enormous group of Anglo customers I rarely saw in our segregated school. Ninety-nine percent of our teachers were Hispanic and bilingual. The evening experience at the drive-in encouraged me to speak English. Both Maggie and Estela, perfectionists in their own way, were having their own issues learning to adapt to the best way to articulate the language spoken by the Anglo customers.

During the very busy evenings, customers rushed in and were eager to get their orders completed, pay for their purchases, and return to their cars to view the coming attractions. The process was maddening. Night after night, we dealt with the same frantic scenario.

One particular evening, a pompous customer rushed in. He was about to turn a good evening into a miserable one and Maggie was a sitting duck. He impatiently looked at his watch as to give her the clue that he was timing her. He insinuated that he demanded to be served rapidly.

The tough customer ordered two hot dogs from Maggie and one large box of popcorn. Maggie politely asked him, "Sir, how do you like your hot dog?" The cowboy annoyingly responded, "Hot." Ignoring his idiocy, Maggie pleasantly responded, "I know sir, do you want mustard and ketchup?" He rudely responded, "No! I want it plain. You should know by now. I come here every week." He was stubbornly holding up the line. He went on to tell Maggie that he wanted extra salt on his popcorn. She curtly responded, "Sir, the salt shaker is on the counter." By this time, Maggie was freaking out.

Dealing with intimidation and humiliation was not one of Maggie's strong suits. I could see that her face was red with anger or embarrassment. Whichever it was, she attempted to hurry his order so the line could move faster. He was finally served and exited the concession area. We needed to learn to serve at a faster rate.

Ten hectic minutes later, the cowboy returned. Maggie was barely recovering from her first traumatic encounter with him. Within seconds, the *'Hopalong Cassidy'*, was in Maggie's face. He barked, "I am insulted and angry and I need to speak to the manager. You have done this on purpose. You should be fired." For once in her life Maggie was speechless.

Responding to the manager's call, I quickly walked to the customer and asked him in what way I could assist him. I always liked that word. It made me feel like an assistant. The man was stammering. Starring at me, he repeated, "I want to see the manager. Are you the manager?" I confidently replied, "Yes sir, I am the **only** manager in the theater."

I had learned to expound my importance and I was going to stand by my sister. At that time, the idiot reached inside his paper bag and produced two cold buns without the hot dogs. The cowboy drawled very seriously, "**I as'ed dis meskin' girl fer two plain hotdogs an'I get two col' buns without the hot dogs. I wanna see the manager.**"

Maggie was about to explode. She hurriedly walked into the back room and started slamming boxes. Surely, she was ready to beat the hell out of the cowboy. Suddenly, she slapped herself. Apparently it was her mistake and she didn't know how to deal with it. To make the situation right, I gave the cowboy two warm hot dogs. Finally satisfied, he went on his way and left us alone.

After intermission, we started cleaning our work areas, as usual. Even though he was gone, we were left feeling minimized and inferior. Maggie was so angry that she told me she wanted to quit- to never be in a place where she would ever be called 'Meskin'. I thought to myself; "Good luck my precious sister- Good Luck."

Estela, in her thoughtful and resolving style, said to Maggie,"Hermanita (dear sis'), at least the fucking cowboy didn't call you a **dirty** 'Meskin'." We laughed vigorously and treated ourselves to three hot dogs each, with everything on them.

The intensity of the moments previously experienced, led me to address acts of intimidation and insolent treatment from customers, or anybody else. This was the aftermath, when I realized that I had to learn that even though the world is full of good people, inescapably there are also bastards out there. I was beginning to realize that if I wanted to make something of myself, in order to preserve my integrity and my dignity, my obligation would be learning how to cope with idiots, by not allowing them to tear me down.

After taking a day to think, I spent a couple of hours, reviewing ways that we could make our system better, for our customers and ourselves. When we started our bi-weekly debriefing, Estela had already taken the 'high road' by focusing on how we could convert a negative experience into a positive outcome.

Estela presented a large colorful poster, that she had designed herself, which included every item on the menu for customers to study before they ordered. Maggie added large letters to the poster with an illustration of a hotdog decorated with various condiments.

Estela and Maggie were elated when they received a note from Mrs. Poag, which congratulated them for their artwork. Mrs. Poag asked them to make a copy for the *Ceniza Drive-In* and paid each of them $5. Thrilled, Estella made a big deal out of her reward. She bragged that her artistic talents were finally being appreciated.

CHAPTER TWENTY

I Know You Found a Happy Home

Dad, this letter is to thank you for the memories of kindness I have of you. Last week we read a poem in our Sophomore English class that made me think of the many fun things we did together. The author lost his mother when he was eight years old, and later lost his dad when he was eleven years old. I was eleven years old when I lost you.

In his poem, the author, writes about memories of his days with his father as they walked though nature- the way we used to walk by the river and the meadows we used to know. He also writes about the way nature reminds him of his dad when he was alive.

I am including some of my favorite lines we read in class: "There was a time when meadow, grove, and stream, the earth, and every common sight, to me did seem appareled in celestial light."

Dad, whenever I was with you walking through the river banks, this is how I remember you now. The other lines that bring pleasant memories of you are: "The Rainbow comes and goes, and lovely is the rose...but yet I know, wher'er I go, that there hath past away a glory from the earth." These line are my favorite because I am sure that even though you have gone from me, you will always be with me as long as I remember you.

I also like these lines; "Our birth is but a sleep and a forgetting; the soul that rises with us, our life's star, and comes from far,...not in entire forgetfulness and not in utter nakedness, but trailing clouds of glory do we come from God, who is our home..." Finally, I wept for you when my teacher asked me to read these lines: "Though nothing can bring back the hour, of splendor in the grass, of glory in the flower, grieve not, rather find strength in remains behind".

Dad, I know that I will see you again. Knowing that you went back to your home and knowing that someday we will meet again, I feel better. I will again be there with you to tumble in the green grass. After this week I won't cry any more or be sad for you.

Dad

Two weeks after I had submitted my homework on memories, our wonderful semester with Mrs. Pasley came to a bittersweet end. Before we said our goodbyes, or 'hasta luegos,' to each other, Odelia Vela abruptly asked everyone to please wait for three minutes.

Evidently Maria de La Luz, Abigail Zapata, and Mary Treviño, had prepared a thank you and farewell card, signed by the entire class, for Mrs. Pasley. It read:

"Though nothing will bring back the hours you have shared your wonderful knowledge and caring for us, we will not be sad, instead we will find joy and appreciation for knowing you as a loving teacher that will live in our hearts forever."

Mrs. Pasley was so touched that she cried.

As soon as all of the students left, mom walked in. I was certain that I was somehow in trouble again. Mrs. Pasley had asked mom to meet with her for a brief conference. She graciously greeted mom and asked mom to sit next to me. Mrs. Paley asked mom how her other children were doing in school. Mom, though feeling uneasy, was proud to say that they were doing fine.

Within moments, Mrs. Pasley addressed mom and clarified the reason why she had asked her to meet with her. Mom anticipated that something awful had happened. Mrs. Pasley spoke:

"Mrs. Carvajal, you have a very intelligent son. He is one of the best students in my class and I want you to know that I admire Antonio very much. He has outstanding writing skills. He writes with rare and uncommon sensitivity- the best I have read in a long time. I just want you to know that I hope you do everything you can to see that he gets into a good college someday. He will most likely graduate next year. This is the year he should be selecting the college he wants to attend. He will be successful anywhere he goes."

Hearing what Mrs. Pasley had to say, Mom cried and hugged me after thanking Mrs. Pasley for being a wonderful teacher. Mom told her this was the very first time she had ever been called to be congratulated for doing a good job on behalf of one of her children.

CHAPTER TWENTY-ONE

I Walked Alone

One night after I delivered the necessary reports to the Rita Theatre late at night, I was enjoying the sensation of success I felt after another day had been accomplished. I had been tired and frustrated by numerous class assignments, on top of, on-the-job challenges with demanding customers.

The walks I took back home by myself, provided me with time that I needed, not to plan for the next day, but to reminisce about the parts of movies I had been able to watch during the evenings at either drive-in. I forced myself to recall verbal encounters between major actors. I learned English vocabulary words from songs and dialogue. I memorized confrontations, love affairs, and choreography which was used to make scenes more true to life.

There were several times that songs from musicals, some of which that had been my favorites, enhanced my appreciation for the versatile talents that the dancers and singers presented.

One of my favorite movies was *Margerie Morningstar*-with Gene Kelley and Natalie Wood. A song from the movie, *A Very Precious Love*, buried itself deep in me, evoking an appreciation for both actors. When the main characters fell in love during a particular scene, my dream was that someday I would find a girlfriend that would dance close to me.

I enjoyed the solitude of my late evening walks, but even if I didn't, I was still the only person that would walk the short stretch from the theatre, confidently crossing the bridge that separated the city of Del Río and my community of San Felipe. It was seldom that, so much as a passing car, would be seen that late at night.

I could sing as loudly as I wanted to, without worry of whether my voice would offend anyone. One particular night, I burst into song:

"A very precious love
Is what you are to me
A stairway to a star
A night in Shangrilá of ecstasy."
Since no one could hear me I made up some of the lyrics.
I even pretended to hear applause

I commonly shifted from one song to another. Another song that captivated me, during the still of the night, was a song made popular by Frank Sinatra, *I'll Walk Alone.* My brother, Ramon, played it on our portable 45-rpm disc player over and over again when he returned from the military service. I remember how he would hum the song, not with a sense of pessimism or regret. but with a note of deep loneliness. This was typically the way our older brother, Ramon, always was- deeply lonely.

I began my next performance:

"I'll walk alone, because to tell you the truth.
I'll be lonely, I don't mind being lonely,
when my heart tells me you are lonely too…"

My singing subsided gradually as I approached a short bend that would lead me into the darkest portion of my journey. Although I was not typically scared of the dark, it still produced a sense of fear within me, every time that I walked there alone. I had made this trip many times before with my mother on our way back from the theater, but making it alone gave me a feeling of vulnerability.

Something about the darkness made it easy to recall memories that had been experienced, in and around, the river during the day time. Although it was my sanctuary, the river had also proven itself capable of taking lives under certain circumstances. It was sometimes hard to forget the severe accidents or fatalities that had occurred there.

As I walked along on one particular night, I had a sensation overcome my body. I felt like somebody, or something, was watching me. My mind twisted and turned with worried thoughts, but I refused to succumb to fear. As I continued walking, I was almost certain that, at the very least, I was being pursued by shadows.

My paranoia got the best of me. I had the uncontrollable inclination to walk faster without seeming alarmed. As I increased my pace, I was also convincing myself even more that I was being followed. Determined to resist falling to fear, I began contemplating various scenarios in my mind.

The river was my sanctuary. I've said it before and I'll say it again. If I was being followed by something, no matter who or what it was, if it was planning an assault, I would simply jump off the bridge. I would dive into the river that I know so well, disappearing into the darkness. I knew where the tree trunks were peering out from the water, how deep or shallow specific areas were, and I doubted that a pursuer would know any of the same.

An untrained person would simply crack their head on the tree trunks or rocks. I believed I could navigate the river and shores blindfolded, which would make for an easy escape in the water. I could swim away like a shark to hide in the dark places that I knew would be safe. In many ways, I felt adventurous, heroic, and proud.

My mind continued rolling at a mile per minute. I was almost starting to hope that I would have the opportunity use some of the many Tarzanian tactics I had learned when exploring all areas of the river with my pals.

Suddenly, looking down under the bridge and seeing nothing, forced fear into reality. The river was pitch dark. Even I would be foolish to jump into total darkness. My only choices left were going to be walking faster or running like a rabbit.

With curiosity consuming me, I had to turn around to see what was following me. In an instant, a man grabbed my left arm. In a moment of terror, I jerked my arm from his grasp, trying to scamper away like a frantic monkey. He lunged at me again, grabbing me by my arm and neck. Like a fish, I effortlessly slipped away from his control for a second time and ran.

I had never run away from anything before in my life. I knew that this time was different, so I ran towards home. I figured if the man was going to continue following me, that I knew exactly where to go to lose him in my own territory. I knew my space. Running was my strong suit; a good thing too, because it became my only means to get away from him.

As soon as I reached the embankment of the river, about eighty yards from my home, I jumped down to the edge of the water, hoping that he would also jump. I knew where the rocks, boulders, mud-holes, and loose dirt would stop him more permanently. The plan didn't work. He fell flat on his face next to me at the bottom of the embankment, but still had enough energy to reach out and grab me.

Holding on to me as tightly as he could, the idiot slurred "where's the money?" He must have followed me from the drive-in. He reeked of dead fish and booze. He had my throat clamped so tightly in his fingers that I couldn't even talk. I wanted to ask him why he was doing this to me.

He grabbed my head and aimlessly started banging it against a large rock. He lacked coordination and was swinging my head wherever he could. A rush of warm fluid came streaming down my eyes and face, obstructing my already hindered vision. It became clear to me that the man did not intend to stop. I didn't want my mother to find me this way. The pain was intolerable. Every beat of my heart throbbed through my head.

I had lost hope. In a moment of miraculous luck, the boozer began gagging and choking. He tried to lift himself up. It was at this point that I realized that he was vomiting uncontrollably. Seizing my window of opportunity, I slipped away from him. With whatever little energy

I had left and with my veins surging with adrenaline, I scurried up the embankment like a wild cat.

I had escaped from enemy territory. I was out of the strangers reach for the moment and I knew that he wouldn't be capable of climbing out so easily. I frantically ran towards my neighbor's house. I started yelling as loud as I could, "HELP ME! HELP ME!!A MAN WANTS TO KILL ME!" Mr. Barrera, who was a well-known sheriff and friend of my family, yelled to his wife to bring him his gun.

By the time the Sheriff came to my aid, the stranger had already disappeared into the night. Mr. Barrera must have called the pharmacist after I fainted. That night, I was treated for deep wounds to my head, shoulder, arms, and nose.

The dawn of a new day arrived and I was still alive. A doctor had come to check on me. My brothers, sisters, dogs, cats, and even Jackie surrounded me with love. My mother embraced me and I fell sleep in her arms. The doctor charged mom five dollars for the house call and left. It was obvious that I was not going to be attending school that day.

That afternoon when school was dismissed, word of the incident had already spread like wildfire. My sister Maggie opened the door for anyone who came to visit. Most of my classmates showed up at the same time. I was given 'get well' cards, popcorn, hot dogs, and cakes as tokens of their sincere caring. Their affirmations stayed embedded in my soul. I even felt loving kisses from my special girlfriend, Romelia. The abuse perpetuated by an idiot suddenly felt worth it.

Five days had passed since my traumatic experience unfolded. Mr. Barrera officially declared to my mom that the suspect was apprehended and arrested. It turned out that the fishy-boozer was stationed at Laughlin Air force Base. The military system would deal with his crime. The next day in class, I was nominated as 'Most Likely to Survive.'

CHAPTER TWENTY-TWO

An 'aha' Moment

My aunt Manina, who had always been like a surrogate mom, constantly asked me if I was doing okay in school. On a weekly basis, she inquired if I was completing my assignments on time. Annoyingly, she would commonly ask me when I was planning to stop living like her four cats, each of which had lost several of their nine lives.

I thought Manina was being funny. I asked her, "Why are you saying that?" It was the first time I heard that cats had nine lives. She explained, "Tu quieres hacer todo. Siempre occupado. Siempre brincando a todaspartes. Te vas a enfemar." ("You want to do everything. Always busy jumping from one place to the other. You are going to get sick.")

I had never pictured myself with having a feline temperament. Having several cats around our house, I knew the various tempers and self–centered dispositions of cats well enough. We had our share of dogs and cats throughout our childhood years. They were all over the neighborhood, scampering here and there- from tree to tree. Somehow, they seemed to realize that our home was a shelter for homeless dogs and cats.

I lived my days overwhelmed with commitments. The more I realized that Manina was right, the more I was convinced that there had to be a way to alter my layers of commitment. I had to make the best of the two years I had left in high school.

CHAPTER TWENTY-THREE

I Welcomed My New World

To reduce my commitments, I first decided to cut back from my routine 42-hours-per-week as a concession manager. I was overwhelmed with work, considering I was also a student for 7 hours per day. The transition was a form of renaissance. My new schedule was humane.

I began to work only on Tuesdays, Fridays, and Saturdays from 4pm to 9pm and every other Sunday. My schedule finally allowed me enough time to focus on my school assignments and gave me opportunities to socialize with my favorite crew on the evenings that I was free.

The crew

Our favorite nights were the nights we spent at the State Park, casting our fishing poles into the deep blue waters and talking about our future plans. When we got morbidly bored, we would go out and buy watermelons and snacks. After that, we simply drove around our community, from one end of town to the other.

We enjoyed driving around and singing love songs we heard on the radio. In some instances, romantic relationships inevitably evolved. My friends; Delma, Richard Chapa, Junior, Nelda, Joel, Diamantina, and Estela were always eager to get on board the, fun and love 'boat,' on Wednesday nights.

Even though I always looked forward to our evenings together, Maggie convinced me that I should be more involved in school activities. She believed that participating in various school clubs would be a way for me to meet other students and get to know my teachers better. One evening, she even took the time to list the various options available; leather and wood crafts, Glee Club, sports, theater, and musical classes.

Other than attending sport activities with my brothers, Joe and Ramon, the rest of the ideas were foreign to me. I had hoped that swimming would be an option. If it was, I believed I would be a super star in swimming and diving. I would surely have qualified for the U.S. Olympic team and been successful. I felt so confident in swimming and diving that I knew I could honor my school with a handful of Silver and Gold Medals. Unfortunately, swimming was not an extracurricular option.

I always hoped and prayed that there would someday be a reachable dream out there waiting for me. Because my older brother, Ramon, had joined the Air Force, I had no one else to guide me in social or school activities. I relied solely on my brother Prieto, who was constantly pushing me towards sports. I was impressed that he wanted me to be like him. He thought he could get me involved in football or boxing twice a week. I was pleased with the idea.

One afternoon, Prieto convinced me to go with him to try out for football. I was a blatant failure. The coach was honest enough to inform me that I was too skinny. I had to gain some weight, because the uniforms that he had available were too large to fit me. I had to work out to develop muscle tone.

Prieto asked him if I could try out for baseball. Entertaining the idea, Coach Piembert asked me to run around the field to test my agility. He specifically directed me to step on a line, get ready to start running at the beginning of a whistle, and to run as fast as I could. I ran as violently and vigorously as my legs and lungs would take me. When I got within forty yards, I almost passed out. Coach asked Prieto if I was a smoker. My brother stared at me and asked, "Are you?"

We walked back to the bench, where the coach flatly denied me. The entire ordeal was becoming demeaning. I wished Prieto would just let me disappear, allowing me to be whatever I wanted. Excluding sports. He was getting ridiculous and he wouldn't quit. This time he desperately asked coach if there were any sports or sport activities available for kids like me. I wondered what 'kids like me' was supposed to mean.

Coach Piembert immediately suggested that I could try out for water boy. I didn't quite understand what that involved. Coach explained, "The responsibility of a Water Boy is to provide water to football players during their breaks. The task involves filling bottles with water, placing the bottles on a tray, making a run to the middle of the field, water the boys, run back, fill up the bottles with water again, and wait for the next call. That's all."

I counted six steps to complete the process. I knew I could do it successfully, so I accepted the position. The following Friday, during a real football game, Prieto was pleased. Even though I felt awkward, I was proud to be at the same stadium that my brother made two touchdowns in.

The following day, I explained to Prieto, that I was quitting because I felt that my skills in athletics were way above being a mere water boy. I knew that even my younger brother, Raul, could do that. I told him that I was looking for real challenges. Prieto was totally speechless and confused- very confused. Some folks would probably call my attitude a form of denial, but for me, on that particular day, I was protecting my self-image.

My school buddies were always good to me. They knew the politics and nature of the high school environment. They knew me as a music man. They had heard me singing loudly while cruising around town on Wednesday nights. They were seriously impressed that I could remember and recite the lyrics of, song after song. I knew almost any song that they requested to hear.

Some evenings, my buddies even challenged me to unfold my musical talents. They dared me to stop the car, get my guitar out of the trunk, and sing love songs. We would park our cars a few yards away from our girlfriend's homes, walk to the windows, and romantically serenade them. These were the girls that we wanted to someday marry.

I only knew three songs. I knew parts of many songs, but appropriate songs for serenading a sleeping beauty were; *Amoricto Corazon*, *Crei*, *Los Dos*, and Joel's favorite *Mucho Corazon*. The first summer, after the word got out, we became known as the Trio Miercoles (The Wednesday Trio). We were on a roll as far as popularity went.

During the very first debut of serenading, two narrow-minded neighbors reported us for disturbing the peace. That was the kind of insult that generally offends the self-concept of any emerging artist. Even though the insult was hurtful, I still considered the experience to be a positive one. Unfortunately, somebody reported us a second time, so we decided to give up the late-night serenades.

CHAPTER TWENTY-FOUR

An Unwelcomed Message from America

After numerous efforts to find the social, athletic, and musical experiences I had sought, nothing I attempted gave me the fulfillment I had been seeking. Even though there were times when the hint of feeling like I belonged seemed to be enough, it did not turn out to suffice.

Something was missing. In many ways I was disappointed that I had left my employment at the drive- in three months ago. I missed the excitement and the challenges dearly. I ended up applying for a part time position as a special usher for the balcony at the *Rita Theatre*. The following week, I was hired.

My role as an usher was dreadfully boring. My main duty was to merely direct kids of various ages to their designated areas in the theater. The theater manager, Abe, was on a temporary job training program from another city when I started my position.

When Abe met me for the first time, he asked me if I was officially employed. I thought he was kidding. I simply couldn't answer. Later, he carefully instructed me that in case no one had informed me, the upstairs balcony in the theater was designated for black kids.

I was puzzled by Abe's instructions and I wondered. My brother Prieto was sort of dark brown. During the summers, after spending twelve hours by the river under the scorching sun, his skin shriveled and got as dark as chocolate. Mine did too.

The first week of my new employment was monitored by 'King' Abe, a twenty-three year old Anglo man. He was simply wrapped up in self -importance and proud of his job as the, on-duty 'captain.' I wondered how in the world Mrs. Poag, the most generous employer I had ever known, got stuck with him.

I was pretty sure that Abe had landed from some nearby planet. Two Saturdays later, he caught me violating his law. I had allowed one of the black kids to use the downstairs water fountain. Abe stood next to me and walked me through the seating regulations, for the third time, reiterating the importance of keeping the black kids upstairs. It was definite.

Standing in the lobby for over thirty minutes, with nothing to do, was an experience I had never known before. I had picked cherries under the hot sun, collected trash from the grounds at the drive-in, directed cars with my flashlight to available spots, and even learned to make popcorn while dealing with cowboys who wore all kinds of hats.

This was exceedingly different. My duty was simply to direct the dark-skinned kids with my flashlight. My flashlight was fancy and it was the only part of the job I liked. I enjoyed shining my flashlight on my face, making funny faces, and playing 'peek-a-boo' with them, as they made their ways upstairs. Eventually, they learned that the lighted-monster was a friend, whose job it was to help them find a place to sit.

The theater played a variety of shows. The cartoon shows were long and loud. Jungle movies lasted about 60 minutes. My simple responsibility was to sit on the balcony stairs, monitor bathroom and water breaks, while waiting for the movies to end.

The kids enjoyed their Saturdays, but I hated mine. I did not, for the life of me, know why anybody would worry about where the kids sat, or which bathroom they should use. There was a restroom for the boys and one for the girls. They were also upstairs. The kids had the entire balcony to themselves. There were thirty seats available, but at most, only ten were ever used.

I explained to my miniature customers more than once, that if and when they had to go to the bathroom, they had to tell me. It was during the moments that I uttered those words, that I embarrassingly wondered why in the world they had to be confined to the upstairs area. I felt a repulsive truth. It was the first time I ever witnessed segregation of this magnitude. In hindsight, it was even more repulsive that I ignorantly participated in the process.

During one 'sleepy time' afternoon, it must have been nap time for me. Abe, the officious manager, had caught one of the kids downstairs again in the 'Whites Only' area. He brought the kid to me with his hand tightly clutching his arm. He tapped me firmly on my shoulder. He immediately and seriously accused me of doing something illegal.

Abe firmly reminded me again, that the kids with dark skin were not allowed to use the restrooms downstairs, or even go to the concession area. He preached, "These kids have their own area. Can you remember that?" It must have been a rhetorical question, because he didn't wait for an answer. He continued his lecture, "We do not allow them to wander around in any other part of the theater. That is why we hired you."

Abe mockingly asked me, "Anyway, why are you here?" It must have been another rhetorical question. He continued scolding me, "Don't tell me that you're employed here. You are violating a serious law. You shouldn't even be here."

The conversation obviously wasn't over. Abe restated, "They use their own water fountain and their own bathrooms." He berated me and asked, "What are you doing here?" Having witnessed my scolding, the kid stared at me and stammered an apology, "Su, me go tinky." I hurt for him. I also hurt for me.

I took the recently released child by his hand and assured him that It was not a big deal. I made a funny face for him, giving him the hint that I was his advocate. I asked him for his name. In barely a murmur, he uttered, "mu Cogu." I thanked him and assured him that he was a good boy.

I took Cogu by the hand and led him up the stairs. I rubbed his head, telling him to hold my flash light. "Sit on the stairs and wait for me," I said, "me candy for you." I went down the stairs to the main lobby and bought one piece of candy for each of the seven kids in attendance. They waved at me as I walked back to my designated stair for people of color. That was my last day on the job. That was the day when the world I had known, turned ugly.

CHAPTER TWENTY-FIVE

Time to Call It a Day

Three weeks had passed since I abandoned my disgraceful position as an usher with a flashlight. After that, I knew I had to move my agenda forward- and quickly. I counted the weeks until my Junior year would pass. I continued having a sense of shame for being part of the ugly experience at the *Rita Theatre* with the kids. The incident continued to provoke anger and shame.

Richard Chapa, Junior Arredondo, Arnoldo Chavarria, Joel, and I always managedto do something with nothing. On our lowest days, we managed to shake off the boredom, by going swimming at our famously favorite spot by the creek, known to us as 'blue waters.'

The trip to our creek was a miserably long walk. We tried short-cuts and long curves. We even walked over the railroad tracks to make our walk more exciting. We hoped to experience a closer look at a thunderous, roaring train, as we walked. We had taken this same route before and only once, had seen a train go by.

One afternoon, as we took our boring walk, Richard halted us, warning us that he noticed four empty box trains were visible roughly a hundred yards from our path. Due to his interruption, we had quieted down enough to be able to hear the voices of adults and children. We heard arguing, yelling, and laughing. We hid behind mesquite bushes and secretly watched like cowboys, reenacting what we had seen so many times in the movies.

Junior pointed at three kids that were running in circles around the box cars. Suddenly, I thought I recognized one of the children. I was pretty sure I had met him at the theatre. We walked closer to their camp to get a closer look. I wanted to make sure it was really him.

We got within 40 yards of the train cars. I was now certain. One of the children was my little friend, Cogu. The same one who I had allowed to break the law. I excitedly shared with my friends, "I know him, his name is Cogu. He is a good kid." I told my friends that he was one of the kids that went to the movies at the *Rita Theatre* on Saturdays.

Our conversation took a different turn. Observing what was before us, I felt inclined to say, "I'll be damned. So this is where he lives? In an empty box train?" I wondered to myself, 'Why here?' I didn't know why they were hiding from the rest of the kids in my barrio. I wondered if they were being separated from the rest of the kids. I kept wondering why. I also wondered where they went to school.

Following the observations of that day, with so many questions running through my mind, I was determined to go back home and tell my mom and my sister Maggie. I started to explain to mom, as calmly as I could, that we had seen a very dark family by the railroad tracks. I took a breath, and as I tried to continue, however her response was brief and to the point, "No te importa" ("none of your business").

During the following weeks, I was struggling with some of my class assignments. At the beginning of the Fall term of my Junior Year, my advisor enrolled me in a typing class that almost killed me. I wasn't used to maintaining a posture for typing. My hands were better suited for catching fish. My fingers did not move in the rhythm that was required.

I was, however, determined to be able to type my own written assignments. Miss Calderon was also determined. She was the kind of teacher who would keep us until 6pm if she thought it was necessary. I realized, that was the discipline I required.

Within three weeks I had successfully learned the key board. After another three weeks of practice, I could type quiet proficiently. Lines such as, 'all good men do fine' and 'this is the time for all good men to come to the aid of their country' must have been typed over a thousand times. 'Wow!!' I thought. I had practiced over and over again, until I could type without even looking at the keys. I was proud that I had met Miss Calderons' criteria.

The Spring term was upon me. My next challenge was a class with Mr. Paz. My friends had warned me, that even though he was an excellent teacher, he required quality work from his students. They spoke of the rigor of his grading system, both in class assignments and the term papers he required at the end of the term. I was pleased. This is exactly what I had been looking for.

On the first day of class, Mr. Paz walked in with a professional, but friendly, composure I had not seen before. He was a proud and meticulously dressed teacher who conveyed uncommon appreciation and regard for his students, from the very minute he introduced himself.

Mr. Paz was also very clear in letting us know that he knew our families well and that he knew where we lived. For me, that established an immediate warning that we had to comply with his expectations of us. It also gave indication of the nature of the content of his class.

I was overwhelmed by the course syllabus. Each component was clearly defined; assignments, grading system, office hours, quality of work expected, and attendance were carefully outlined. Mr. Paz spoke firmly, "I have to stress to you that written assignments must be submitted when due- you cannot miss class, or be late. If you miss class and you tell me that you were very sick, I'll go by your house and ask your parents the date and hour you were admitted to the hospital." At that moment, three of my friends and I felt doomed. We exchanged frightened stares with each other.

Mr. Paz's tone softened. He spoke clearly and sincerely, "I welcome you to a terrific journey that will take you through many aspects of the law of our country, our supreme Law- the U.S. Constitution." I had been preparing myself for another boring experience. This new encounter was going to be anything but boring. It was going to be the key to my future.

Mauro Paz

The first week of Mr. Paz's class, he lectured us on the reason why we had a Constitution. He taught us about a time in history when several individuals from thirteen states agreed that King George III of Great Britain was oppressing the freedoms of the colonized people. As a tyrant leader, he commanded the people to follow his rules.

Mr. Paz, in his simple and sincere manner, explained a very difficult phase of American History, which captivated us with his knowledge. He made us laugh when he broke the ice by quoting lyrics from a popular song we had heard, *Hit the Road Jack*.

King George III, lusting for his own power, demanded to get whatever he wanted. Arturo described him as the 'King Kong' of England. After a long list of abuses and unyielding oppression, the colonized people had simply had enough. Fed up, they demanded that he hit the road.

Thirteen colonies felt that they had no choice but to move forward and find a way to earn their own personal freedoms. Roberto Chavira made me laugh when he told me that the people from England finally told the tyrant King George, 'No Way Jack. We are outa here.'

The people from each of the original colonies decided to form a union for themselves. Enough was enough. The people declared their independence from Great Britain on July 2nd of 1876. The treaty was ratified on July 4th, which has become our Independence Day.

Mr. Paz explained to us that the introduction to the Declaration of Independence, later known as the Preamble, embraced the principles and values that guided the writers of the manuscript. Thomas Jefferson, with the collaborative participation and guidance of the state representatives, drafted the document known as The Declaration of Independence. The signers of the declaration would become there presentatives of the thirteen new states.

After the celebration of freedom, representatives from each of the states realized that they had another major task to accomplish. They were compelled to avoid the nature of the tyranny that they had experienced under King George III. They had to establish new laws that would guide their new citizens.

At this point, Mr. Paz read the most exciting and patriotic message, I had ever heard, in a flawless and dignified manner:

"We hold these truths to be self-evident, that all men are created equal, that they are endowed by their Creator with certain unalienable rights, that among these are Life, Liberty, and the pursuit of Happiness. That to secure these Rights, Governments are instituted among Men, deriving their just powers from the consent of the governed. That whenever any Form of Government becomes destructive of these ends, it is the Right of the People to alter or to abolish it, and to institute New Government laying its foundations on such principles and organizing its powers in such form, as to them shall seem most likely to affect their Safety and Happiness."

After his eloquent reading, Mr. Paz explained to us why the new country had to establish the guidelines for the new philosophy, emphasizing the aspects of equality for all, personal rights, life, liberty, and the pursuit of Happiness.

Mr. Paz stressed that because the concepts embraced by the Declaration of Independence had to be addressed, the next challenge would be to define how these significant mandates could become a respectful guide for the people. He was pleased that this urgency was addressed by some of the same individuals who drafted the Declaration of Independence. Their document was entitled the Constitution of the United States.

The newly created Constitution of the United States included sets of rules and specific laws that would govern the new Nation. The new challenges and proposed changes had to address the principles defined in the Declaration of Independence.

Mr. Paz convinced us that The Preamble of the Constitution, specifically cites the philosophies embraced within the context of the document:

"We the people of the United States, in Order to form a more perfect union, establish justice, insure domestic tranquility, provide for national common defense, promote the general Welfare, and secure the Blessings of Liberty to ourselves and our Posterity, do ordain and establish the Constitution for the United States of America."

Mr. Paz stressed that the founders believed that the purpose of the Constitution was that it would be the instrument that would guide the lives of Americans for future generations.

CHAPTER TWENTY-SIX

Scholarship

Each day we met, Mr. Paz intrigued us with other phases of the development of the Constitution; the arguments, disagreements, the compromises, and most significantly, the changes that were made known as Amendments to the Constitution. The Amendments were most significant because of the impact they already had made on our lives.

Mr. Paz stressed that the changes amended into the Constitution would significantly alter the fiber of America. That was the part that intrigued me the most. For an in-class assignment, he instructed Robert Chavira and I to work together on writing the biography of Abraham Lincoln.

Mr. Paz, in his organized style, prepared a schedule for class presentations. He allowed two class periods to allow the pairs of students time to review and discuss the content of our findings, while preparing for the presentation. We had to remain in the classroom or work in the library. He would monitor the groups and give advice if needed. It wasn't that he didn't trust us, it was just that he didn't trust us completely.

Roberto was involved in football during these mester of the assignment, so he asked Mr. Paz if we could be first to present. I was surprised that he had the gall to tell Mr. Paz that he had to be at football practice on some afternoons. Mr. Paz firmly declined. At that point he made it clear to the class that every single student had to be present for all presentations. Not even water boys could be excused. No excuses were acceptable. That made me feel good. Nevertheless, we decided to be the first group to present. We had one more day to prepare.

Both Roberto and I took our assignment seriously. The first interesting information we found was Lincoln's physical appearance. We were fascinated at how tall, lanky, and skinny he was. Roberto said that Lincoln didn't look like a president because he came from humble beginnings and generally did not look sophisticated. I agreed, thinking that he looked like someone that would come out of the barrio. I really liked my point. I was a realist.

Soon after the superficial parts of our research, we learned many other personal qualities about Mr. Lincoln and his strength of character. We emphasized that the most important and serious challenge for President Lincoln, was the issue of slavery. Lincoln stood firmly in his belief that the abuse of Black people as slaves was wrong and unfair.

There were several members of Congress who disagreed with President Lincoln because, they themselves, owned slaves. The issue was too explosive and serious for any member of Congress to dare speak against slavery when some members were slave owners.

Climactically, it took a Civil War between states for any change to happen. The states that were in favor of slavery, the Southern states, lost the Civil War and slavery ended. It is sad that so many lives, from both the North and the South, were lost.

We emphasized that even though many people were not happy, Congress passed a law that black people had to be free. This decision was known as the Emancipation Proclamation. Reconstruction of the states began soon after. Resistance from both the Northern and the Southern states created deep animosity. Lack of confidence and distrust of each side started to create political battles all over again.

During this difficult point in history, on April 14th 1865, the 16th president of the United States, Abraham Lincoln, was assassinated. The assassin was a well-known actor and Confederate sympathizer. His name was John Wilkes Booth. The crime occurred at *Ford's Theatre* in Washington, D. C.

A funeral train took President Lincoln back to his final resting place in Springfield, Illinois. The eulogy was delivered by Ralph Waldo Emerson, a favorite poet of mine since I was in the ninth grade. I remembered, all too well, that I knew his literary works because of Mrs. Pasley's assignment. I had learned so much from reading his essays.

The Oration

The following is an address, which was delivered by Mr. Ralph Waldo Emerson; orator, poet, and essayist, at Concord Massachusetts, on the occasion for the funeral services in honor of Mr. Lincoln, in April, 1865:

"We meet under the gloom of a calamity which darkens down over the minds of good men in all civilized society, as the fearful tidings travel over sea, over land, from country to country, like the shadow of an uncalculated eclipse over the plane. Old as history is, and manifold as are its tragedies, I doubt if any death has caused so much pain to mankind as this has caused, or will cause, on its announcement; and this not so much because nations are by modern arts brought so closely together, as because of the mysterious hopes and fears which, in the present day, are connected with the name and institution of America. In this country, on Saturday, everyone struck dumb, and saw, at first only deep below deep, as he meditated on the ghastly blow. And, perhaps, at this hour, when the coffin which contained the dust of the President sets forward on it long march through mourning States, on its way to his home in Illinois, we might well be silent, and suffer the awful voices of the time to thunder to us. Yes, but the first despair was brief; the man was not to be mourned. He was the most active and hopeful of man; and his work had not perished; but acclamations of praise for the task he had accomplished bursts into a song of triumph which even tears for his death cannot keep down. The President stood before us a man of the people. He was thoroughly American...."

After we completed reading the excerpt from the oratory above, to the class as our conclusion, we felt that we had met and known the 16th President of our country. I was deeply touched by the oratory. For some reason I cried on the way home.

During the last week of our term with Mr. Paz, he asked us to write our names on an appointment roster to review his evaluation of our presentation and term papers. Roberto and I set the date and time we would meet with him. The day we were supposed to see him, Roberto called to change the date. He had other pressing family emergencies. Mr. Paz rearranged his schedule to meet with Roberto, but I had to meet with him by myself.

Our grades were 98% for our term paper and 100% for our presentation. He wrote excellent praises on both assignments. We had earned an A for both pieces. I thanked him and told him that I had learned a lot from his class.

After receiving the good grade on our assignment, I stood up to shake Mr. Paz's hand. He stood up, shook my hand and told me to please sit down for a few minutes. He spoke to me, "Antonio, you need to hear what I have to say. Listen carefully. Each month we have a teacher's meeting to discuss text books, class schedules, and teaching resources." I wasn't sure where this was going. He continued, "We also give ourselves time to discuss student academic performance, especially now that we are ending the Junior year."

I was now anticipating the possible reasons he was telling me this. I continued listening as Mr. Paz spoke, "Your name has been an interesting point of discussion. Mrs. Pasley, especially, has shared with the teaching staff at our meetings, more than once, what a remarkable student you are."

I felt very honored to hear that Mrs. Pasley had said good things about me. Mr. Paz continued, "She speaks of your outstanding interpretation of literature, your writing skills, and your serious commitment for scholarly readings. She also has very high admiration in the way you work with your classmates." My pride was blossoming. "She appreciates your leadership in class."

I was modestly embarrassed. I thanked Mr. Paz and told him that I was very glad to hear such good news. As I made a gesture to leave, he stopped me again, asking me to sit back down. He said: "You have been an exceptional student in this class. You have an excellent ability in understanding the legal implications of the research documents you have read and presented to the class."

It was like kind-torture. He wouldn't stop, "I am proud of you, not only because of your work in this class, but because I also happen to come from an environment exactly like yours." I was shocked. I always thought of him as a royal descendent. He explained himself to me, "Antonio, my parents also came from Mexico during the Mexican Revolution- just like your mother and her parents. The struggles that you experienced, I have experienced."

I could still hardly believe what I was hearing. "I know you have struggled with poverty just as I did. Each time you spoke about President Lincoln as he grew in poverty, I could hear and admired your sensitivity. All this and more will take you a very long way. I am going to make a special effort to have a conference with your mother, Chelito, to share with her what I have told you."

'Here we go again,' I thought, 'another conference with mom?' Mr. Paz concluded, "I must tell her that you have to prepare yourself to go to college." He suddenly shifted his speech to Spanish, "Mira, mi hijo, eres oro molido, de un character muy fuerte. A ti nada te tumba" ("Listen son, you are a person of rare quality with a very strong character. You are like crushed gold. It will take a lot to knock you down.")

Mr. Paz stood up telling me that he would see me again in the Fall. He continued speaking as he shook my hand, "The next advanced phase of this course will require more independent research. Each student will research and examine what we have done with the challenges and mandates of both, the Declaration of Independence, and the Constitution of the United States."

Finally, the relentless praise was over. Mr. Paz told me, "I'll be looking for you in the Fall." He closed with a Spanish phrase, "Mientras, por favor, vaya con Dios" ("In the meantime, please, go with God.")

CHAPTER TWENTY-SEVEN

There Simply Was Not a More Congenial Spot

It had been during the last semester of my Junior year, that I realized the intensity of the social aspects of San Felipe. I knew of the various activities that occurred during the final two years of school, but I had never been in the eye of the storm.

I vaguely remembered the academic, social, and royalty honors, that were as real and significant as the days of Camelot. The Knights of the Round Table, love affairs reminiscent of King Arthur and Guinevere, and even the sneaky Lancelot- came to life in a flash.

The halls of our high school wing were bursting with social and romantic excitement. It could have been predicted that a couple, if not several relationships that evolved during that time, would result in forever-and-ever permanent marriages. This reality encouraged me to definitely believe in Camelot.

Because of my work commitments during years past, I was, for the first time, able to appreciate the significance of these days. My peers were beyond ecstatic to be part of the process of any activity they wished. Some were involved in the selection of speakers for graduation, menus for banquets, decorations, locating appropriate places for dances, contracting musicians for dances, and selecting music and songs for graduation.

I had heard of, and seen, the way teachers and editors of the Conquistador magically emulated the hint of royalty and regal flares of the environment, though I had never seen the process used. It was real, the HOUSE of Royalties was bursting all over. It was a wild and chaotic time. I wondered how anybody could prepare for final exams during that time.

I decided to be involved, so I forced myself to be part of the process of nominations for class favorites and any other possible social pedestals. I was eager to compensate for all the times I was unable to be part of social school activities. I was intrigued and fascinated to learn how the process worked. I also learned to admire and respect the abundant dedication of the candidates.

During those weeks, it became obvious to me that the students who were nominated for certain honors, were students with consistent, meaningful, and significant participations in the areas for which they were being nominated. 'The Best All Around,' 'Best Athlete,' and 'Most Likely to Succeed,' were nominations that evolved from the committee of teachers and fellow students. There were other titles such as; 'Most Handsome' and 'Most Beautiful,' which were also nominated by the same committee, but were primarily gifts of nature and good dental care.

There was a Bachelorette breakfast, which I attended with Romelia. Our teachers spent time preparing us for it, by teaching us table etiquettes. Some things we learned were; no elbows on the table, proper use of napkins, and courtesies when speakers were addressing us. We were guided not to talk too much or too loudly at the table, to pull chairs quietly, allow our dates to sit properly, and to not allow our eyes to wander all over the place. We were trained on how to be a proper guest at our table. I wished that mom and Jackie could be there to see what a gallant person I had become.

Maggie had been employed and earned enough money, some of which she used to generously buy me the necessary outfit for our special breakfast. She dressed me up to look like Tony Curtis with a 'Kiss Me Quick' haircut. I looked absolutely awesome- a prince from the land of Camelot.

The Bachelorette breakfast was relevant because of the significance it had on graduation. Other than the elegance and the glitter of the occasion, it was also the time when I realized that a group of my close friends from the class of 1956 were graduating and leaving our school. They were already talking about San Felipe as the past; as their Alma Mater.

The graduating class sang a song, with tears in their eyes, that I had heard, but probably never understood prior to the ceremony. It was a song composed by a dear administrator by the name of Mr. J. B. Peña:

San Felipe School Alma Mater
(Chorus)

San Felipe, Alma Mater
Praise thy name of high
Hail to thee oh glorious High School,
Name that shall not die

CHAPTER TWENTY-EIGHT

Pocket Change Galore

As soon as we left San Felipe, the time clocks disappeared. Our lives began to change rapidly. We were eager to get back to San José; the city of cultural diversity, enormous blossoming plants, and abundant citrus fruits of all kinds. Our favorites plants had always been the clinging Boganvelia vines and Avocado trees in blossom. San José became a dream home away from our barrio.

The succeeding weeks moved rapidly. It seemed that even our seven day weeks were tapered to one day. Raul, Francisco, and I worked five days a week, detailing cars at the same detail shop we had worked at for the past three years. We worked by harvesting crops on weekends. We knew the art of field work and knew where the owners were fair and where the orchards were plentiful.

That season, I managed to get a job at a Del Monte cannery from 9pm to 7am. It was a difficult shift, but a tolerable place to work. When I received my first pay check, I suffered a small stroke. It was a stroke of happiness. I was in a place where I was paid more money in one week, than I had ever earned in half a year.

Perhaps even better, my friends; Joel and Richard, who were from my barrio, were also working on the same shifts. It was amazing that we were here, over two thousand miles away from home, all working together at the same place. Also, the better pay was a bonus.

After two weeks working weekends in the cherry business, I gladly surrendered my ladder to Raul and Frank. They were pleased to fire me as their supervisor. They worked hard and didn't need me to watch them do it. I was pleased to have a more lucrative salary elsewhere anyway.

The last Friday and my last day working at the orchard, I was day-dreaming, thinking, and talking to myself out loud. I suddenly saw a lovely looking, older lady, who was waving at me from across the fence. She was near the property of some building that was still in construction. I had seen her before, but this time I realized that she was admiring the way I could jump from branch to branch and reach the highest branches.

Before the day ended, during my lunch break, I saw the lady unpacking boxes from the trunk of her car. I jumped the short fence and simply walked over to her. She was mildly startled but seemed pleased to see me. She addressed my approach, "Hon, goodness, you're here to help me?" She gestured and pointed towards me, "I think I know who you are." Suddenly the light bulb above her head illuminated. "You are the gifted trapeze artist that jumps from branch to branch."

I remembered seeing the woman at this orchard during the previous season. I was surprised that she also seemed to remember me. She reintroduced herself, "I am Miss Gibson. I will be a teacher at the college here starting in the fall of next year."

Miss Gibson was a part time teacher during the previous season when I saw her for the first time. It was strange coincidence that I saw her here again. She questioned me, "Are you from this area?" I replied, "No, I am from a barrio in San Felipe, Texas." I continued to share, "My family and I have worked here for three summers." I would have continued conversing with her, but was running short on time.

"Can I help you?" I asked and then I expressed my urgency, "I have to hurry up before my two bosses get back from lunch." Miss Gibson introduced herself again, "Remember, I am Miss Gibson and I will teach Speech and English classes next year." Then she asked me, "Are you interested in school?" I told that I was already graduating from school. She responded with a sweet voice, "No, I mean this building will be a Junior college.

Miss Gibson started probing me, "Do you plan to go to college?" I immediately responded by telling her that my family didn't have money. She abruptly intervened, "No, you don't need money to go to school here. It is free for two years…after that you go to a bigger college in the city." I was becoming interested when she said, "Listen, I have to go too." She handed me some papers with her name and phone number.

I was about to go back to my cherry picking when Mrs. Gibson added, "Three months before you graduate from high school, call me or write to me and I will help you select a program." She offered, "Maybe next week if you have time, I'll show you a map of how the campus will look." I immediately told her that this was my last day working here and thanked her for being such a nice person to me. She was truly one of the kindest persons I had ever known.

It was very difficult to start thinking about leaving San José. My social life with friends was incredible. The environmental majesties I had found while exploring the vast horizons of beaches, mountains, forests, and green pastures where everywhere we went. I could not have predicted such beauty- not in my wildest dreams.

It was clear to me why so many families decided not to return to San Felipe. They made this gorgeous San José their home. I was even tempted to remain in my newfound paradise. Never-the-less, completing high school was a promise I made to myself. It was a promise I had to keep for myself. It was important to finish it, in the presence of my family, for my future.

CHAPTER TWENTY-NINE

Un Mundo Raro
(A Rare World)

My brother, Frank, decided to stay in San José with Raul. The rest of us returned home, making our last year in San Felipe as livable as we could. Mom, Maggie, and I had enough funds to repair and remodel parts of the house.

Nothing seemed to be the same any more. Jackie, my long-time faithful pony had grown and left. Perhaps he went on to find his own way or he had been tired of waiting. Golon, the puppy factory, had taken off as well, hopefully to a better home who had a family that also accepted her wayward ways.

Our little mascot, Payito, was now entering third grade at the Escuela Amarilla. Mom decided to go back to work at *Kress*. She continued enjoying her Tuesday evenings after work at the Spanish Cinema, although without me. Payito became my permanent replacement.

I admired Mom for her participation in musical productions. She worked alongside Mr. West, a school music teacher. She was the main pianist and conductor of musicals that were performed by high school students. Her music filled her with glory and I was going to get all of the glory I could out of my last short months before graduation.

My aunt Manina was now the manager at the drive-in and was enjoying the limelight and responsibility of her position. She was a real trooper and was also well known for cooking the best Chile Fritos in the entire Southwest.

My brother Ramon married a lovely woman, Mary Ellen Ramirez, who was from Dallas, Texas. The couple said their vows shortly after he completed his Bachelors of Science Degree in Engineering from *Southern Methodist University* (SMU). He was fortunate to have been able to cover educational expenses with the Veterans GI Bill.

Our lives had changed greatly since I had returned. Now I was entering a new and rare place. The world that I knew, would be mine for a brief time- and then pass. I had to make the best of it.

The first week of my senior year, we had the usual school assembly. The administration welcomed us, introduced the new teachers, and heralded us as the class of seniors that would be graduating in eight months. That sounded very final to me. I was glad to see my favorite teachers; Mrs. Pasley, Mr. Alanis, Mr. Paz, and others. They were the educators that I had been privileged to; have, know, and admire, before I left for my summer work in California.

Mr. Martinez, our stern and unyielding principal, read a list of rules and expectations he had also read during the beginning of every semester prior. Word for word. Nothing new and nothing exciting. As he read, my mind immediately took me to 'la la land.' It was a place similar to my river dream land, but now I went back to the oceans, beaches, blossoming vegetation, forests, and new friends I had met during my stay in San José. I yearned to go back.

Teno Flores prodded me to wake me up. He warned me that Mr. Martinez was starring directly at me, "Wake up. He'll call you to the office to see him." When the school bell rang, I dragged my feet out with the rest of the Juniors and Seniors, who were undoubtedly also dreading another year.

Our first hour seemed like a boring eternity. During lunch time, most of the seniors drove off in their own cars. It seemed that several of the guys that had gone to California, or other states, had saved enough money to buy their own cars. That's how I had gotten mine.

We brought back the huge *'Batmobile'* Lincoln that was piquing the admiration of my peers. I even had enough pocket money saved to buy the gas needed to cruise around each week. By the second week, we were getting ready to get serious about school, pass our classes, and begin thinking of moving on.

My first morning class was scheduled at 8:30am with Mr. Paz. That was a boost to my otherwise dormant existence. When I walked in, the classroom was packed. There were only two empty chairs. Arturo had been saving space for me and asked, "Where in the hell were you?" He told me Mr. Paz had already called roll. "He called your name. I told him you were parking your huge boat across the street." I wasn't sure that I found that funny.

There were twenty eight of us in Mr. Paz's class. It seemed that the same group of us who were Juniors in the Spring, were now Seniors. We kept our agreement with Mr. Paz that we would return and enroll for the second phase of the American History class.

Before we had ever left for our summer break the previous year, Mr. Paz had challenged us to realize that the second phase would require us to examine the impact of the Declaration of Independence and the U. S. Constitution and the influence they would have in our personal lives. He noted that it would bear more significance, especially in three years when we became adults at the age of 21. I turned to Arturo and commented, "That sounds absolutely weird. We are adults?"

CHAPTER THIRTY

In Search of New Paths

Shortly into Mr. Paz's course of increased intensity, there were Bill of Rights presentations and discussions. Moving right along, our group was later assigned to address the plethora of Amendments. Even though we felt prepared, the content was surely going to prove overwhelming.

On the morning of our presentation, I decided to walk a short cut I used to frequent. It went through the river embankment and made for a quick walk to school with Roberto Chavira. Both of our homes were in the poorest area of town.

During that particular morning, Roberto asked me if I had plans to go on to college after graduation. My response was nil. "No coins no nothing," I said. I was glad he asked though. I told him that I met a lady on top of a tree that had promised to pay for my college.

Roberto was ecstatic over hearing that someone was going to help me get through college. He thought it was great. "If she lived on top of a tree, was she a bird?" he asked, laughing and making fun of me, "Do you plan to live on a tree?" I explained to him more clearly how I had met Miss Gibson. I ignored the rest.

I told Roberto that college could be easy for him because he could get money or scholarships from colleges to play football- just like Prieto did. He wasn't acting too sure about it. I shared with him that I wanted to be a lawyer like Mr. Paz, because he knew all kinds of laws. There was Mrs. Pasley too. She read all kinds of books. He reassured me that I could do either because I liked school.

It felt really good to be talking about graduation. "By the way," Roberto said, "Mr. Paz is not a lawyer…but he should be." As we started getting close to school, we started running faster. We only had four minutes left to get to class. He had to be in class with Mrs. Pasley.

As we made our approach, standing there in front of the building, was someone that looked like one of our teachers. Sure enough, it was Mrs. Pasley. She was standing by the street as if she was directing traffic. She waved to Roberto and asked him to stop for a while. I attempted to continue my walk. Mrs. Pasley requested for me to wait for Roberto.

I thought that surely, Mrs. Pasley must be angry. She spoke firmly and sounded disappointed, "Roberto. Listen. You have been late to class several times and have not turned in your work for **three** assignments." She added, "You seem to have time to get to football practice, but not for completing your school work." She was obviously quite peeved with him. "Next time, I will talk to your parents." She sternly finished the conversation by saying, "Now, class has started. You need to be there right now." I felt good knowing that she cared so much. Roberto was puzzled over it, but he seemed grateful too.

That morning in my class, Mr. Paz's lecture addressed the day that Congress had passed the Civil Rights Act, which demanded the equality of all men before the law. The act called for fines and penalties for anyone found denying patronage of public places, such as theaters and inns. The Supreme court did not accept this. The Supreme Court attempted to turn the tide against the Civil Rights movement.

The resistance of the Supreme Court on the subject of the Civil Rights Act, for all practical purposes, resulted in previous legislation and amendments being ignored. A 'Separate but Equal' clause was their way to get around the issue. That basically meant that segregation could continue as long as the facilities for black people were equal to the facilities of white people.

So long as both whites and blacks had their own water fountains, their own railroad coaches, and their own restrooms, they could remain separate. That was the deal. The Supreme Court upheld that as long as the facilities were equal, blacks could be legally segregated.

The loophole that the Supreme Court used to bypass the Civil Rights Act gave me an overwhelming and emergent need to share the experience I had at the *Rita Theatre*. I recalled my memories of when I had been hired part time, as an usher, on Saturday afternoons. I could still hear 'King' Abe's voice, "Black kids cannot use the restrooms or water fountains downstairs because that area is reserved for white customers." He also had said, "These kids have a designated area upstairs, because that is exactly where they belong." To top it all off, he insisted, "Blacks are not allowed in the main area of the theater. They have their own facilities."

I then understood what the "Separate but Equal" clause meant. It was a way to abide by the law, allowing the kids to enter the theater, but to segregate them. So long as the facilities were equal to the facilities for white customers, they could continue separation to their heart's content. I found that to be such a deceptive way to get around the Civil Rights Act.

After recalling my past experiences so vividly, I decided not to share with the class. Due to my respect for Mr. Paz, I decided to share the horrible details with him privately after class. He extended his hand to me, shaking it, and thanked me for sharing.

Roberto and I been assigned to research the 14th Amendment. We informed the class that our term paper included an important message: By 1950, black Americans were beginning to challenge segregation in the public schools and that their parents had won five separate court suits. Because of that, American public schools were compelled to change.

The following day, the content of the 14th Amendment seemed impossible to unfold. As much as our groups read, discussed, and reviewed the content, the more difficult it became to understand the many implications it carried. Mr. Paz yielded us, asking my group to respond to questions of the class. He advised us to share as much as we could and reassured us that he would help in areas that we could not answer.

An inquisitive classmate, Dolly Martinez, wanted to know how long a person had to be a slave, what kind of work they did, and how much they got paid. After Dolly initiated the first question, the class continued participating with, nonstop and relevant questions.

Mr. Paz reminded us to answer each question, one at a time. Vividly recalling another past experience, I once again avoided sharing it with the class. It was my memory of the segregated 'home' where Cogu lived. I thought it would be awkward, mostly because I didn't have an explanation. I thought it was cruel to segregate over ten people in an empty box train.

I was having a difficult time, truly rationalizing the segregations that I had witnessed. Scratch that, I don't think I understood at all. I also remembered how I felt about the theater not allowing my cousin Estela and her friend to sit wherever they wanted. That wasn't freedom, rather blatant discrimination. I began to realize that it was impossible for me to deny that segregation and prejudice existed. Terribly, it was more common than I wanted to admit.

As if experiencing a painful revelation, I was beginning to have a sinking feeling. For some reason, the violation of the 14th amendment, which forbids the denial of life, liberty, and the pursuit of happiness to anyone- was being blatantly ignored. No one seemed to care.

Before class was dismissed, Mr. Paz first challenged us to focus on a very important section of the 14th Amendment. He read the significant message for us cautiously and sincerely, "In addition, it forbids any states from denying any person; life, liberty, or property without due process of law- or to deny to any person within their jurisdiction equal protection of the laws." He continued, "The legal definition of 'due process' is clarifying for us that fairness is a fundamental principal in a legal matter, both civil and criminal, especially in the courts." His closing statement was, "All legal procedures set by statute and court practice, including notice of rights, must be followed for each individual so that no prejudicial or unequal treatment will result."

Our next class with Mr. Paz inspired us, truly making us feel like young adults. He expressed his admiration to each of us for our commitment to become self-disciplined and self-reliant. He cautioned us that the years ahead would be filled with enormous challenges, as well as some disappointments, and trials. He confidently expressed that he believed that each of us had the ability to endure whatever our near future had in store for us.

Mr. Paz addressed our class, "Most of what you have learned in class; the amazing history of our country, the values of the people we learned about, and even about the suffering and struggles that so many African Americans endured, will be important to remember throughout your personal journeys."

Mr. Paz delivered great praise for African Americans, "They had the survival skills and the moral strength to move forward." We felt inspired by his speech, "In spite of blatant treatment of discrimination and oppression, they had the fortitude to lift themselves from nothing." We were so enthralled that we didn't want class to end, "Your parents did the same, and so will you."

As class was coming to a close, Mr. Paz confided in us, "I will tell you something else before you go. I am only your teacher because of my parents." He had us in great anticipation of what he would share next, "When they arrived from Mexico during the Revolutionary War, they carved a road for me that would bring me to where I am today." He delivered a sweet conclusion, "You know your parents have been carving a future for you also. Your gift to them shall be your commitment to become the best that you can."

I couldn't contain the emotions evoked by Mr. Paz. I shed tears of love and gratitude for my mom and dad's unconditional care of my brothers, sisters, and me. Even Mr. Paz had tears in his eyes. He gave us one moment of silence. The class applauded him. Many of us reached out to him. Some embraced him and others shook his hand.

Abigail and her sister, Rachel, were both shedding tears of pride. They said to Mr. Paz, "We're going to tell our guelito (dear grandpa) what you told us." They emphasized, "He will be so proud of you. He and my parents also came from Mexico."

While he was collecting his materials, Mr. Paz reminded us that the next day everyone had to empty and clean our desks, and definitely, prepare to vote for our favorite candidates. He spoke again, "As a parent would say, you need to be prepared to look your best on next Saturday for your graduation." He reminded us, "All of your teachers will be expressing their admiration for each one of you, for what you have become and accomplished during the four years you spent with us."

Now was the time that an enormous, class-made, purple and gold card that expressed the caring, love, and gratitude we had for such a gifted teacher, was presented to Mr. Paz by Dolly Martinez and Odelia Vela. Their words, wrapped in a profoundly sincere message, evoked tears from an amazing teacher that will always be in our hearts.

   The next day was bittersweet. It was the last day of classes. Mr. Paz returned our graded notebooks and handed out the graduation letters he had written for us. It was undeniable how much he valued and cared for us. I knew that he was definitely a teacher I would never forget.

CHAPTER THIRTY-ONE

Barnum and Bailey Would be Appalled

Every single corner of the school was bursting with activity. This day was the most casual of Fridays. Students and teachers were behaving more like friends than mentors and pupils. A group of teachers and students, stood in line to vote for their favorite candidates. They were exercising the examples of 'due process' that we had learned that year.

Another group of people was in charge of making purple and gold streamers, while another was busy completing copies of our graduation song. Yet another very large group was patiently standing in line for a, well-deserved and delicious, lunch. There was enough for every student and teacher. Parents, grandparents, and aunts and uncles, had prepared enough tamales, chili-beans, and rice to feed an army.

Students who were graduating and I were busy practicing our procession march in the auditorium. The next day we would practice on the field where we would ultimately receive our diplomas. Teachers were reviewing protocols of courtesy with graduating students and student hosts that would welcome their parents and guests.

By the time the busy day of preparations ended, some of the students and parents were so exhausted, one of the school bus drivers offered to take all of them home. When everybody was on board they proudly waved goodbye to parents and students that were left behind.

To their dismay, the bus refused to start. Sadly, Everyone, one-by-one, had to get off the bus and walk or get a ride home. The next day would prove to be filled with an equal amount of madness. It would start all over again. The environment was safe. The teachers would go back to acting like professionals again. Students were quite proud, but also sad that the end was in sight.

CHAPTER THIRTY-TWO

Begin the Beguine
"Volver a Empezar"

On the day of graduation, I was living a nightmare at our home. Mom had started to pack all of our belongings for a permanent move. Nothing would be left behind. Anything that we could not take would have to be given away. Sentiments of goodbyes to dogs and cats were not permitted.

In her usual manner, she pushed us to clean the patio and sweep the rooms before we were to depart in three days. What an eccentric expectation that was, I thought. No one would care how we left the house. Even if somebody did, it certainly wouldn't matter to us.

I was required to make a trip to *Red and White*, the grocery store, to get more boxes. Ismael, the meat market adviser and good friend, informed me that mom had already been there three times, taking all the boxes he had. He directed me to go to the Sanchez's grocery store. I soon discovered that Mom had already been there too. I wondered how we would even be able to transport more than twelve boxes.

During the madness of our preparations, Mom yelled at me to find my cap and gown and shine my shoes. I found one shoe and the graduation gown, but not the cap. She demanded that I try the gown. It fit just fine. I looked outside, noticing that one of the cats was playing with my cap. I rushed out, got my cap, and ran back inside telling Mom that I had found it. She asked me to try my gown again. It still fit.

Mom told me to get the iron ready so that she could press my gown. In her wild desperation, she took the iron and frantically started pressing it. A piece of the gown got stuck to the iron, tore away, and left a huge hole on the upper left side of the gown. My heart ached for her when she started to cry. This was the first time in a very long time, if ever, that I heard her sobbing.

Thinking quickly, I ran out of the house to see if our neighbor Chonita was home. She usually sewed items for Mom. I carefully and calmly explained and described the terror of the situation. I always saw her as patient and calm, having nine kids who commonly shared our river. She didn't disappoint my impression. She grabbed her sewing basket of threads and needles and followed me home. Mom was now resting though she was still in tears.

Doña Chonita was a saint. She consoled Mom, telling her not to worry. Within thirty minutes she had removed some cloth from the inside of the massive sleeve of the gown and made a pocket in front of the gown to conceal the hole. It looked simply stunning. Doña Chonita had saved the day.

I had to be on the school grounds by four o'clock to practice our procession for one final time. I gathered my graduation attire and walked to the river where I would stay for more than an hour. I refused to put myself through another chapter of agony.

After relaxing as much as I could by the river, I headed to the school. Half of the graduating class was there already. When I arrived, I could see mom and all my family looking absolutely grand. It was time to start the dance of our lifetime- the fantastic dance we had been waiting for, for so long- The Beguine.

It wasn't too long before my nosey buddies noticed the pocket on my gown. They asked why I had it. Before I could respond, my cousin Estela, who was also graduating, told everyone that only honor students had a pocket on their gown. The rumor spread like wild fire. Students were amazed and impressed, making me feel even more grand than I did before.

The bittersweet graduation ceremonies lasted three hours. The silent and serene evening, the echoing of the soft sounds, and the melodies and voices filling the air, conjured memories of the days we had been together. We were even writing farewell notes to each other.

Suddenly, before I knew it, the band began the drums and instruments for our marching procession to return to our families. This is when tears happened. As soon as I met Mom, I hugged her and thanked her. She wept again. I knew that she was proud of me.

Invitations to graduation parties were distributed by the parents of graduates. Mom was firm and insistent that the only party that Estela and I could attend was the party hosted by my aunt Caro and her.

CHAPTER THIRTY-THREE

A New Reality

We left for San José the day after graduation. Our sparkling, clean and reliable, Lincoln allowed us to arrive in two days without any delays. By the time we had arrived, we had solid plans as to what our next phase entailed. Finding a reasonable place to rent was our first priority. The second priority was to find jobs that paid well.

We were lucky to find a rental property that was available for one month free of rent if the, to-be-renters would agree to paint the entire interior of the house and make minor interior repairs. We jumped on the deal. That allowed us a whole month to find jobs.

We immediately returned to field work on weekends to earn enough funds for the immediate expenses that we had before us. In the interim, I found another job at the Del Monte Foods cannery for a night shift. My shift started at 10pm and ended at 7am. It was like I was reliving the job I had there the previous summer.

During the succeeding afternoons, I addressed my next priority. I returned to the building site of San José's Junior College to register for part time, late afternoon classes. During my second visit to the campus, I recalled the advice that the wonderful lady Miss Gibson had extended to me before I left to complete my high school diploma.

Miss Gibson had encouraged me to contact her as soon as I returned from Texas after graduation. She had particularly stressed that the tuition was free. After three unsuccessful days of trying to locate her, I decided to check the college directory. She had moved her office and classes to a new wing on the campus.

Even though I had learned where Miss Gibson had relocated to, it still took me five days to make contact with her. One Friday afternoon, as I was walking to the cafeteria, I saw her walking towards me. She immediately recognized me as well. She invited me to have lunch at the cafeteria.

Little did I know, that lunch at the cafeteria would be the beginning of my career. Today, I still value the importance of having known her. After two meaningful years at San José Jr. College, with Miss Gibson as an advisor, I earned an Associate of Arts Degree that made it possible for me to transfer to any four year college, of my choosing, as a Junior. Even the sixty hours of general requirements would be waived.

I suppose I had many options, but I decided to transfer to San José State College, where I started a Bachelors of Arts Degree program in English literature. I was fortunate to attend a college that happened to be only three miles away from home, however my experience at San José State College would soon prove to be my academic defeat, rivaling that of Napoleon's defeat at Waterloo.

I foolishly continued working evening shifts at the cannery, making it seem nearly impossible to meet rigorous academic requirements. I knew I had made a huge mistake by continuing the night shift at the cannery, on top of declaring English as a major. We were required to read a novel each week. I attempted to read the assigned literature, but falling asleep was much more enticing.

My aptitude in English composition was proving to be dreadfully weak. I struggled to meet the scholarly standards that were required of me each time I completed essays and term papers. Each time that my written assignments were returned to me from my professors, the usual negative grades and comments were devastating; 'Syntax and grammar are at an elementary level- unacceptable, This assignment cannot be read nor graded, Citations are awkward and scattered,' or even, 'Please make an appointment to see me.'

The worst comment I ever received was, 'In the mean time I suggest that you contact advisors from San José City College that can guide you to choose a non-academic major that leads to manual occupations.' This was the killer. I simply refused to make an appointment. Even though I managed to do well in interpreting the readings and oral presentations of American and English literature, it still was not enough.

My most prominent problem was my use of grammar and methods of composition. After the first semester of classes, I was placed on academic probation. This merciless status signaled the beginning of the end of my education at San José State College. By the end of the second semester I was suspended from San José State.

I was at my lowest ebb in life. I simply could not carry on. Even my physical health had been seriously compromised. One afternoon, on the way home, I collapsed on the city bus. The bus driver called an ambulance and I was admitted to the emergency unit. My family was frightened, but also at a loss as to where they could turn for assistance.

The evening of my collapse, my sister Maggie, and Mom, decided to call my dear cousin Berta, who had also grown up with us in Del Río. She happened to be a nurse at a hospital in San José. Berta thoughtfully and dutifully came to the rescue. She called my brother Ramon in Dallas. Without hesitation, Ramon pleaded for Berta to purchase a one ticket for me- to fly me out to him in Texas.

Ramon picked me up from the Dallas airport. He and his family were so gracious, offering to care for me, which ended up being for six months. While in Dallas I was diagnosed and treated for a severe case of Mononucleosis. I had a condition that was caused by fatigue, exhaustion, and undernourishment.

My stay in Texas was incredibly restful. The loving care I received from Ramon's wife, Mary Ellen, his two daughters; Anna and Elenita, was exactly what the doctor ordered to put Humpty Dumpty together again. I felt like a new man. I was grateful for the special care and hospitalities that nursed me back to health.

When I returned to San José, I was able to find a job at *Macy's* department store. The job was exciting, but the hours were long and the pay was minimal. I knew that I couldn't continue this way. We had too many financial commitments at home.

On one late Saturday night, while I was waiting for my bus to take me back home from *Macy's*, Mr. Paz's inspiring words coursed through my mind, shaking my morale like a ton of bricks. I could almost hear him talking, "A ti nada te tumpa, cuando vas por los suelos te levantas. Yo se que puedes siguir tus suenos." ("Nothing knocks you down, when you hit rock bottom, you manage to get up, press on, and follow your dreams.")

Six months had passed since my recovery. I was prepared to continue. Arturo Cuellar; my best friend, mentor, and the same boy who was a member of my private tree at the Escuela Amarilla during the third grade, urged me to apply at a school he would be attending. At *Sul Ross State College* in Alpine, Texas.

I decided not to share my intentions with my family. Within two weeks I requested an admission packet to apply to Sul Ross. Two weeks after submitting my inquiry, I received the application for admission. It took me, what felt like the entire duration of three days, to gather all of the information that was required.

I meticulously filled out and submitted the application. I silently waited with tremendous anticipation for positive news. Over a month had passed, but finally after the fifth week, I received a letter of acceptance. I felt ecstatic and a complete sense of triumph.

After the registrar in the admissions office completed a thorough evaluation of my transferrable credits from San José junior and state colleges, I was informed that I had to complete three more semesters to obtain a Bachelor's of Science Degree in Education. I would need a major in English literature and a minor in speech and language. I thought I had died and gone to heaven.

I couldn't keep my secret any longer. It was time for me to share my plans with my family. They were very sad over the thought of seeing me go, but remained happy for me, which was well illustrated by their support. Two short weeks later I started packing and sorting necessary academic papers from both colleges I had attended.

My family's support was extremely positive. Every one of my brothers and sisters contributed advice, whatever funds they could donate, and snacks for my trip to Alpine. With tears in her eyes, my sister Payito gave me a gift that she had wrapped herself. It was a Christmas candle I would treasure forever.

I left for Alpine, Texas on Christmas Eve to prepare for the Winter Semester. Mom prayed for me the entire day of my departure. She gave me her Catholic blessings when I left. Arriving in Alpine, so far from home, was not easy. I had to find a place to live, recruit roommates, and secure a part time job.

My first semester at *Sul Ross*, was better than I had ever expected, however, my finances continued to impede my ability to afford my living expenses. I was feeling dreadfully irresponsible for not being able to provide any assistance to my mom and my siblings back home.

When the second semester of my first year at *Sul Ross* was about to begin, I finally decided to call my brother Ramon. I rambled non-stop like a blubbering idiot, "Ramon, I completed my first semester with a 3.8 GPA- Alpine is a terrific place- it's a mountain place where the buffalos roam- Sul Ross has excellent professors- They actually talk to you." Finally finding the courage to reveal the reason for my call, I said "Ramon, this is the deal. I need two more semesters to complete my program. I need to ask you for a $300.00 loan to cover my tuition for next semester." I could still hear myself rambling when he interrupted me, "I am proud of you. The girls are always asking for 'Ding Dong.' I'll send you a money order in three days." He asked for my address and then insisted that I visit them sometime soon.

I felt so relieved to be able rely on Ramon's loan. After hanging up, I suddenly felt like a rude and callous moron. I realized that I hadn't even asked Ramon how my little angels, Anna and Gigi, were doing. My sweet little nieces had nicknamed me 'Ding Dong' during the time that I was recuperating in their home in Dallas. They used to play with me, ringing an imaginary doorbell and saying, "Ding Dong," when they visited my bedside.

Ramon and Mary with their two daughters,
Gigi and Anna

The second semester began. With Ramon's loan, I was able to register for 18 more semester credits. I also began to work at the College library and at a local grocery store. I felt like I was experiencing a miracle. After that, there would be only one more semester, which would entail supervised student teaching. That would complete my program.

The year wasn't over yet and I refused to think of how the last semester would happen financially. Some people live from day to day, while I lived from semester to semester. During the uncertainty of the in-between weeks, I just took deep breaths. I uttered Mom's usual "Valgame Dios" ("Oh my God,") when things got really tough.

Evidently, during my first year at Catholic school, two of my favorite Nuns had inculcated the spiritual concept of a miracle. They inspired me to believe that fervent prayer, so long as its wholesome and sincere, can get us through difficult times when nothing else seems to help. This was obviously a good time for fervent prayers. I would simply hope for the best.

Three weeks before the second semester ended, I dragged my feet to a seminar, which I was required to attend. It was conducted by my educational advisor, Dr. Prude, where he discussed student teaching placement for the following semester. This would be the final phase of my program.

It had always been an excellent experience during any opportunity that I could see Dr. Prude. I had already completed two previous classes with him. He was a fantastic professional and a genuine human being, however the morning of the seminar, he was not very humane.

Dr. Prude addressed his audience, speaking in great detail of the specific rules, policies and expectations we had to respect in our roles as student teachers. He announced, "You will be placed in a high school with a mentor teacher who will instruct you through your day." He was rigorously firm, "You are expected to be there when they tell you and leave the building when you've been excused." His voice sounded like a recording of the law, "If you are absent more than twice you have to start the experience with another supervising teacher." He warned us, "If you fail the second time, your program will be terminated."

The gravity of the situation held me firmly stationary. It was at this point that I saw my hands trembling and felt a twitching sensation in my eyes. I could even hear ringing in my ears. I seriously wondered if I was going to pass out. I believed that the task would be impossible. I had no transportation, new clothes, shoes, or even groceries.

I knew that I would not have enough time to work after my student teaching except on Sundays. After school was out, I would have to develop lesson plans, practice instructional techniques, and grade papers. I would even be responsible for writing discipline plans to address academic and behavioral problems as they occurred.

After forty five minutes of Dr. Prude delivering my death sentence, he separated the class by academic majors. Each student would be required to meet with their advisor at their office within fifteen minutes. I could not remember the name of my English major advisor, or where his office was located, to save my soul. I couldn't even remember my name.

What seemed like out of the blue, I heard a voice speaking to me. I knew it was a real voice. It said, "Tony Carvajal, you have an appointment to meet with Dr. Shelden at 3:30. I will be there also." I hurriedly left the room to search for Dr. Shelden's office.

No matter how hard I tried, I was not able to find the office. I felt it was a scam. I thought I was going to be kicked out of school forever. I guessed that I could go back to California to pick cherries.

Finally, I realized that I had gone to the wrong building entirely. I paused my frantic search, sat on a cement bench and reviewed my notes. My calendar notebook where I kept my important schedules was blank. My quivers started all over again.

As I started walking the perimeter of the library building, I saw Dr. Prude enter a building across from it. I ran after him like a rabbit, attempting to take deep breaths to conceal my rapid and erratic breathing. When I caught up with him, I saw him entering an office. The sign on the door indicated that the occupant was, 'Dr. Andrew Shelden: Chairman- Department of English.'

When I walked in, I immediately recognized Dr. Shelden. He was my professor for two of my English classes. I always read his affirmative comments on my assignments several times. He made me feel intelligent.

Dr. Prude spoke to me first. He introduced me to Dr. Shelden as, 'Mr. Carvajal.' I felt honored. Dr. Shelden offered me coffee or orange juice. "No thank you sir," I courteously declined. What I really wanted to cure my hysteria was a cinnamon roll or a burrito. As the blurriness wore off of my vision, I started to examine his impressive office. It was meticulously lined with books from wall to wall.

Dr. Prude continued to address me, "Mr. Carvajal, a recruiting team from Eagle Pass, Texas, was here last week hoping to recruit three high school teachers- two in history and one in English." I wondered why he was telling me this. He went on to say, "I nominated you for the English position." My jaw hit the floor, "Dr. Shelden and I have reviewed your academic résumé and he agrees with me, that you would be an excellent candidate." I was praying not to pass out.

Dr. Shelden confidently explained, "Even though you have not completed your requirements for your Bachelor's Degree, we are allowing you to complete your student teaching on a Provisional Certificate." The wonderful man had me dumbfounded. I finally had enough nerve to speak, "Sir, I think I like what you are saying and I am flattered, but am also confused."

Acknowledging my concern, Dr. Prude responded, "We are saying that if you accept this contract, your student teaching requirement will be waived." He went on, "In other words, you do not have to report to your assigned school, to start your student teaching next fall." I was stunned as he continued, "In essence you will be paid a regular teaching salary from the Eagle Pass School District, all at the same time you will be completing 15 hours of student teaching."

I was in heaven. Such an opportunity had to be the miracle I had fervently prayed for. Dr. Prude concluded, "This is what we refer to as a 'Paid Internship.' At the end of the school semester, if all goes well, we will recommend you to the State of Texas Certification Department to receive a teaching certificate." Then came the icing on the cake, "At that time you will also be awarded a Bachelors Degree from this college."

I felt like I was choking on my own excitement. "Dr. Prude, am I understanding this?" I asked. He proudly responded "You bet you are, Mr. Carvajal. You came to us highly recommended by your professors, including Dr. Shelden." Dr. Sheldon added to the conversation, "You are ready young man. You are ready to go out there and turn on the lights for young high school freshman, like you once were yourself."

Dr. Prude took the floor again, making an additional speech:

"Also, I must add, you are also highly recommended by a person that knows you very well. This person knows you for your very fine character and stability and believes that you will rise to the challenges you will find in the educational system. Her name is Evelyn Poag. She was your employer and mentor for some years while you were attending San Felipe High School and working at one of the drive-in theaters."

I almost jumped from my chair, "My gosh! My precious friend!" "How is she?" I asked. I requested, "If you see her, tell her I send my best regards and that I am thankful for her recommendation." I explained to Dr. Prude, "She was always there for me and my family. My brother and sister also worked for her."

Listening to our conversation, Dr. Shelden chuckled. He urged Dr. Prude to share the other 'good news.' My curiosity was piqued. Dr. Prude proudly shared that Mrs. Evlyn Poag was his wife. He elaborated, "Mrs. Poag's previous husband, Mr. Paul Poag died a few years ago." He proudly announced, "Mrs. Poag is now Mrs. Prude. We got married five years ago."

My heart was standing still. This was the beginning of a super, major miracle. Life is like a carousel. It goes around and around, eventually bringing people whom we have loved back into our lives. I seriously thought that someday when I have time in the future, or at least years later, I would attempt to write a book about their love affair.

Dr. Prude snapped me back to reality. "Well, let's return to business," he said. He then asked me, "Are you willing to sign a contract with the Eagle Pass School District?" He informed me, "The prorated salary for one semester is $7,500." That was fantastically unbelievable. At that very special moment, I firmly, unequivocally, definitely, and totally believed that at least twelve Guardian Angels had been watching over me.

Dr. Prude summarized, "As you well know, Eagle Pass is 45 miles from your hometown of Del Río where you were born." I quickly responded, "Yes sir! Where do I sign!?" I was looking for the contract on his desk. "Well you have to be present to sign your contract and meet with the Superintendent, Mr. James and his other staff," Dr. Prude explained. "That's only a formality. At this point consider yourself hired." Dr. Prude explained that I had only one more week of classes. Then he asked, "When can you go?" I eagerly answered that I could leave on the bus one hour after my last class on Thursday. I told him that I had an aunt that lived in the city of Del Río.

Before I left his office, Dr. Prude offered to give me a ride to Del Río the following week. That essential moment, I wished I would have realized that this magnificent day was going to be the first step to a forty-two year profession in Education.

After our meeting, I received a congratulatory hand shake from both of my professors. I ran so fast that I tumbled all the way down the hill to clean my apartment and call Maggie to spread the news to the family. I told Maggie, "I will be home for Christmas. No parades please. No drum rolls." Maggie laughed.

I did not head for home immediately. After signing my teaching contract, I went directly to the Teacher's Credit Union and borrowed money to make a down payment on a car. I opened my first checking account, withdrew cash, and drove all the way to Dallas to reimburse my brother for his generous loans. Most importantly, I was pleased to buy a house present for Ramon and Mary Ellen. I brought a trunk full of Christmas gifts for my precious little nurses, Gigi and Anna. I later sent a money order to Mom back in San José. Our days of dire poverty, the way we had known them, were over.

PART THREE
Where We Are Today

My graduating class, 59 years after graduation

Arturo Cuellar

Academic:
San Felipe High School graduate, 1957. Elementary schools: Las Calaveras and Escuela Amarilla. Bachelor of Arts degree: Math, Sul Ross State University.

Professional Accomplishments:
Officer for the United States Air Force. Attended Flight School in Merced, California. Completed B52 Navigator training at Pease Air Force Base in Portsmouth, New Hampshire. Arturo flew 78 combat missions in Vietnam.

Completed IBM Computer training. As a result of his excellent skills and experience, he was given two assignments in London, England-totaling seven years. During those years he was assigned to three Olympic games; Albertville Winter Olympics in France, Barcelona Summer Olympics in Spain, and Lillehammer Winter Olympics in Norway.

Throughout his career, Arturo traveled to 46 countries.

Family:

He wedded a woman by the name of Carolina. He fathered two children; David, a graduate of Santa Clara University in Business, and Lisa, a graduate of San José State University, in Journalism.

Lisa has chosen to serve God within a group called 'Youth With a Mission,' in Europe.

Arturo's parents were Manuel and Francisca Cuellar, both of whom were born in Ciudad Acuna, Mexico. He had three siblings, Roberto, Dora, and Yolanda.

Mary Treviño

Academic:
San Felipe High School graduate, 1957. She earned a Degree in Early Childhood Education.

Professional Accomplishments:
Kindergarten teacher for twelve years.

As of the year this book was published, she and her husband continue Business and Community endeavors.

Family:
Mary's parents were; José Treviño, who was born in Zaragoza Coah, Mexico, and Paulita Menchaca, who was born in Bracketville, Texas. Her siblings were José Teviño Jr, who was also in her graduating class, and Eloisa, her older sister.

Mary Treviño married a man named Joe L. Urby in 1959. After they married, they moved to Lubbock, Texas, where they opened a grocery store. Both of their children, Joe Jr. and Jim Robert were born in Lubbock, Texas.

Mary and Joe's first son, Joe Jr, was born in 1960. Their second son, Jim Robert, was born in 1961.

In 1962, Mary and her family moved back to Del Río, where they stayed for 4 years. In 1966, they moved to San Antonio, where Joe began his career in business.

After working for a company known as *Mrs. Bairds* for several years, Joe was promoted into an administration position as Account Executive. During that time, Joe and Mary purchased a farm in Lytle, Texas, where they farmed coastal hay. When this book was published, they were still baling and selling hay to the public.

After Joe's retirement, he and Mary purchased a six acre property called Antique Village in Divine, Texas. That business involves renting spaces for antique shops, general vendors, farmers, etc. They even added a food court which creates a family atmosphere. People from the local and neighboring communities enjoy each other there. As of 2015, Mary and Joe run and maintain Antique Village with one of their grandsons, Ryan.

Mary's first son, Joe Jr, is currently CEO of a major government contracting company. Joe Jr. has given her three grandchildren; Marlena, Joe Ryan, and John Mathew. All of them have completed advanced degrees in Business Administration.

Mary's second son, Jim Robert, joined the United States Air Force. He was stationed in San Antonio for seven years. He then transferred to Germany in 1993. Finally, he was transferred to Great Falls, Montana, where he retired. He served a total of twenty years in the military. He moved back to San Antonio where he works as a Detection Office Manager of Airport Homeland Security, presumably still today. He and his wife, Sandra, provided Mary with three grandchildren; Kyleigh – 9, Kyndall – 4, and Maverick – 1, as of 2015.

Joe, Mary, and Grandson Ryan

José Treviño Jr.

Academic:
San Felipe High School graduate, 1957.
Bachelors of Arts in education from *Our Lady of the Lake*, San Antonio.

Professional Accomplishments:
During the time he was in high school, José, better known as Joe, was involved in various leadership activities; President and Treasurer of Band, President and Treasurer of Future Teachers of America.

The list of his participation continues: He was also a member of the Radio Club, Square Dance Club, Junior Police, Yearbook Assistant Editor-in Chief. He was also a Co-Assistant Business manager and eventually was promoted to Yearbook Editor-in-Chief. Joe even found time to be a Senior Class Reporter.

It is no wonder that his selection of "Most Versatile" by his graduating class honored Joe with such distinction.

After receiving his degree, he taught High School in San Antonio. After he left education, he enlisted in the United States Air Force until he retired.

<u>Family:</u>

Jose Treviño Jr's parents were; José Treviño, who was born in Zaragoza Coah, Mexico, and Paulita Menchaca, who was born in Bracketville, Texas. His siblings were Mary Teviño, who was also in his graduating class, and Eloisa, his older sister.

Eunice Zapata

<u>Academic:</u>
San Felipe High School graduate, 1959.

<u>Family:</u>
Eunice's parents were Señor José Leon Zapata, who was born in Marquiz Coah, Mexico, and Señora Natividad Lomas, who was born in Del Río, Texas.

Eunice had the following siblings:

Rachel - Class of '57, Abigail - Class of '57, José Leon Jr. - Class of '57, Eunice – Class of '59, Leobardo Abiu - Class of '60, Joel Javier - Class of '62, Ana Maria - Class of '65, Berta Estela - Class of '67, Eliu - Class '70.

Three of Eunice's siblings are deceased: Rachel, Abigail, and Eliu.

Eliu was in the Navy when his ship was docked on the island of Diego Garcia off the Indian Ocean. He drowned at sea in March of

1981. He was a member of the last class that would ever graduate from San Felipe High School in 1970.

Eunice's father taught her and her siblings to speak, write, and read Spanish so they could become bilingual.

Ana is currently working as a bilingual editor.

Joel completed his Master's degree in Bilingual Education. He is a retired school teacher who continues substitute teaching on occasion. His devotion to his students in un-ending.

Leobardo and Señor Zapata served as Presidents of the PTA (Parent Teacher Association).

Eunice's family frequently worked as migrant workers in Gilroy, California, harvesting citrus fruit. Because of their need to meet the obligations of their contracts, they were usually three weeks late returning to school.

Eunice has fond memories of walking everywhere they needed to go when they were children. Three or four of them would walk as a group to the library to check out books. They would eagerly read them so they could return for other books.

Eunice's parents were avid readers in Spanish. They inculcated their love of reading to the family.

Señor Zapata was a self-employed mechanic. Whenever the school bus broke down, the football players, unable to reach their destination, stayed behind. Diligently, Eunice would drive him to wherever the bus had stopped, assisting in any way that he advised. Soon she was riding the bus with the team.

Eunice fondly recalls the caption on her dad's obituary; 'Se acabo el mechanico de los pobres' ('The car mechanic for the poor is gone').

In 2015, Eunice stated, 'What an awesome ending to his life; taking care of his fellow man. He always fixed their cars whether they had the means to pay him or not. We are so fortunate to have been blessed with such wonderful parents.'

In Loving Memory of Abigail, Rachel, and Eliu.

Roberto (Bob) Chavira

Academic:

San Felipe High School graduate, 1957. Selected 'Best Athlete' by his graduating peers.

Bachelor of Arts degree: Chemistry and Physical Education, Howard Payne University.

Master of Arts degree: Administration (Superintendent Certified), Texas A & M.

Professional Accomplishments:

1978-1999, School Administrator: San Felipe Del Rio Consolidated School District (SFDRCSD)

Teacher and Football Coach: Del Río High School.

Teacher and Football Offensive Coordinator for Laredo Nixon High School in Laredo, Texas.

Teacher, Head Football Coach, and Athletic Director: San Felipe Independent School District.

Teacher, Administrator, and Coach for 38 years in total.
Mayor of Del Rio, Texas for Four Years.

Community Involvements:
　　Mayor of the city of Del Río: Four years
　　City Councilman At Large: Four Years
　　President: American Forum
　　City of Del Río Police Academy: Member
　　United Civic Organizations: 34 years
　　Lions Club: Past President
　　Baby Ruth League: Past President

Family:
Roberto Chavira's parents were Jesus Chavira, who was born in Allende Coahuila, Mexico, and Maria de Jesus, who was born in Del Río, Texas. Roberto's parents are both deceased.

Roberto married a woman named Carmen. Together they had six children:

Sally - Reading Specialist, Robert - UT graduate and self-employed, Ruben – deceased, Mike – UPS Employee, Cindy – Teacher for San Felipe Del Río Consolidated School District, and Abel Ray – Six Year Army Veteran.

Roberto had six siblings:

Mario - BA, MA, and teacher for 35 years, Gustavo - BA in Computer Science, Jesus (deceased), Mike (deceased), Dora – BA, and Maria Del Rosario (deceased).

Adriana (Nani) Maldonado Foster

Academic:
　San Felipe High School graduate, 1957. Selected 'Most Popular' by her graduating peers.
　Graduated with honors as Valedictorian.
　Bachelor of Arts degree: Speech and Hearing Therapy (Speech Pathology)

Professional Accomplishments:
　After graduating college, Nani became a speech therapist for the Houston Independent School District and Laredo Independent School District.

Family:
　Nani's parents were Jesus Maldonado and Beatriz. Her father is deceased.

Nani married a man named Richard Edmund Foster. He died on July 14th, 1999.

She had one brother named Gerardo Maldonado. He died on January 7th, 2014.

Richard and Nani had two children together; Delia and Cynthia.

Delia completed a degree in Accounting. She has a seven year old son, Vinny, whom is a very good golfer, tennis player, and also takes piano lessons.

Cynthia is a teacher for children with hearing impairments. She has two children; Foster and Olivia.

Foster is 13 years old. He is on the football team for his middle school. He also plays piano and Stand-Up bass with the school's concert orchestra.

Olivia is 11 years old. She plays the piano and takes voice lessons.

Nani states, "God has blessed me in so many different ways. My daughters, my sons –in law, my grandkids, and my truly wonderful and loyal friends have certainly enriched my life. I may not communicate often with my classmates of '57, but I do think about you and the good times we had during our high school years and how special we were to each other."

Lupe De Hoyos

Academic:

San Felipe High School graduate, 1956.

Lupe attended *Our Lady of Guadalupe Catholic School* until the Seventh grade. After that, he transferred to San Felipe Jr. High School.

After graduating from San Felipe High School in 1956, he attended Texas A & M for one semester, where he then enrolled at Sul Ross State University.

He later attended Monterrey Tech University in Nuevo Leon, Mexico. When he returned from Mexico, he finished his studies at Sul Ross where he was involved in college baseball, track, and boxing.

He completed a Bachelor of Arts degree in Biology and Physical Education.

Professional Accomplishments:

Lupe taught at San Felipe High School from 1959 to 1965 as a biology teacher and sports coach.

He coached his team through three baseball championships; one regional, one Bi-district, and one District.

From 1965 to 1970, he served as Head Coach at the Del Río Independent School District. Once again, he coached his teams through the baseball championship every year.

Lupe started the first Recreation Department in Del Río.

In 1992, he became the Athletic Director for the SFDRCSD.

Family:

Lupe's parents were Ramon de Hoyos and Maria Castorena.

He had four siblings; Sylvia Cullhum, Pete (deceased), Rachel, and Ramon II.

Lupe and his wife, Jessie, were married in 1978, and have celebrated thirty five years of marriage.

Andy Porras

Academic:

San Felipe High School graduate, 1958. Selected 'Best All Around' by his graduating peers.

Andy began elementary school in School #2, known as Escuela Calaveras, and later transferred to School #1, Escuela Amarilla.

Andy attended Sul Ross State University, obtaining a Bachelor of Arts degree in Journalism.

Professional Accomplishments:

Utilizing his degree, Andy returned to San Felipe High School, where he taught journalism for four years.

After his last year in San Felipe, he received a Journalism Fellowship from the Wall Street Journal, allowing him to attend the University of Texas. After meeting the requirements of the Fellowship, he pursued graduate studies at San José State University, where he completed a

Master of Arts degree in Journalism, sponsored by a Mott Foundation Grant.

Andy continues to follow his ambition to write and lecture. Currently he writes for *Hispanic Link* and other publications. He lectures at colleges and universities on the topics of Hidden Hispanic History and Mass Communications.

In 2015, Andy has been reviewing and summarizing a manuscript on a Longitudinal Study of Hispanic educators.

He also recently wrote the Foreword for *The Roads We Traveled*.

Family:

Andy's top priority is spoiling his grandchildren; Jah'Sol Amaru and Star Zehari Alma. He is also busy re-creating Mexican Revolution Posters.

Andy's parents were José and Josefa Porras.

Andy's father was a firefighter at Laughlin Air Force Base in Del Río, Texas and and also served on the San Felipe School Board of Education. He and Andy's mother owned a, very well known 'mom and pop' store, *Andy's Grocery*.

Andy is married to Josie, a delightful woman and friend of our family.

Leo Cardenas

Academics:

San Felipe High School graduate, 1953.

Leo had a head start in education since, beginning when he was four years old. His mother had enrolled him and his sister Odelia, in a Baptist kindergarten- on Garza street. After he graduated from the Baptist school, he was ready to attend either of the 'Ivy League' elementary schools. He attended *La Escuela Calaveras*. His siblings were educated in Catholic schools.

Leo was the only one in his family to graduate from San Felipe.

While in high school, Leo wrote for one of the two school newspapers. This experience gave Leo the opportunity to become the editor of *The Mustang*, the big time newspaper, published every other week by the student council of the San Felipe High School.

After graduation, Leo attended the University of Texas. He earned a Bachelor of Arts degree in Journalism, 1958.

Professional Accomplishments:

In 1960, Leo worked for a local newspaper as a sports editor. A year later, he was accepted by the San Antonio Express Newspaper, where he became Assistant City Editor.

Leo was recruited by the United States Department of Justice, where he became a communications specialist in 1971. Within six months, he served as Special Assistant to the Director of Community Relations in Washington D.C. In 1973, Leo was promoted to Regional Director and transferred to Denver, Colorado.

Other areas of professional accomplishments include; Founder of Sierra Federal Savings and Loan, Chairman for the Board of Latino Broadcasting Corporation, and Chair Member for the City of Denver Personnel Board.

Leo also extended his professional commitments into surrounding community relations:

Servicios de la Raza Board : National Vice President.

League of United Latin American Citizen (LULAC) Magazine : State Director and Editor

Author of *Return to Ramos*, a publication for bilingual education.

Family:

Leo's parents were Oscar Flores Cardenas and Gertrudes Ramo.

Leo is the oldest of five siblings; Olivia, Mauro, Oscar, Issac, and Alda.

Olivia is a graduate of *Sacred Heart Academy*. As of 2015, She lives in San Antonio, Texas, where she enjoys her retirement from the Civil Service.

Mauro is also a graduate from *Sacred Heart Academy*. He is retired and also lives in San Antonio.

Leo's youngest brother, Dr. Issac Cardenas was the Dean of Chicano Studies, but has recently retired. He is an Emeritus Professor at California State University at Fullerton. Ca.

Commentary:

Leo Cardenas is a man for all seasons. When I gleam at the remarkable journey Leo Cardenas has experienced, I am left in awe at the various places and numerous people his life has touched. It was predictable that from the "get-go" his life was destined to move in the direction it was meant to go.

Like many of us, he wouldn't dare miss the roads he was destined to take. Reading and analyzing the specifics of the twists and turns in his life, replications of the San Felipe markers are clearly evident.

The first marker was the element of Faith inculcated by his mother Gertrude (Tules). Mothers of the barrios were powerful in this department. The other element was the evident way that our families remained a team throughout difficult times. We were encouraged to accept our struggles- not to revel in self-pity as the common phrase goes, 'pobrecito de mi, esta vida es major que se acabe' ('poor me, this life should just end.') None of that nonsense. We were taught to treat our challenges as blessings that would carve out our characters for later years. Another consistent phrase, 'Ley de la Tierra' ('Law of the Land') was education. 'Estudia y callate' ('Study and keep quiet'). Simple as that! The final and quite significant element, was his opportunity to be educated by some of the most outstanding teachers from our beloved San Felipe High School.

I was particularly exhausted waiting to see when in the world Leo was going to stop and rest, even if just for the sake of calling it a day for a while. No way. He went on persevering- like a tireless rabbit drumming forward on a lithium battery.

I salute you Leo Cardenas. I am honored to have known you better this time around.

Odelia Vela Reyes

Academic:
San Felipe High School graduate, 1957. Selected 'Best Athlete' by her graduating peers.

Family:
Odelia was the oldest of eight children and also the one responsible to take care of them. Surely it had something to do with why she was selected as 'Best Athlete' from our graduating class. I just imagine seeing her chasing after her seven siblings- day in and day out.

Odelia's mother and father worked diligently to provide for their kids while she was young. Even though they lived in an economically disadvantaged situation, their days in the barrio were characteristic of joyful, and nothing-but-good times, which they enjoyed as a family.

Working in the fields, picking cotton, and sheep shearing, for long months at a time was not an easy task. She recalls that since she was nine years old, the family began canvassing for work in the fields. They ended up harvesting cucumbers and other vegetables in Wisconsin and other states.

Odelia's teenage years were typical of teenagers anywhere in the country. The only difference is that she found contentment and appreciation in simple things. She enjoyed listening to music, doing her hair while her family was on their way to work the fields, letting her feet hang out of their pickup truck, and pretending to be a movie star.

Her teenage years exemplify a person embracing life to its fullest. Throughout her life, Odelia has been guided by a meaningful spiritual philosophy: "God takes care of His own". I am inspired by my amazing friend.

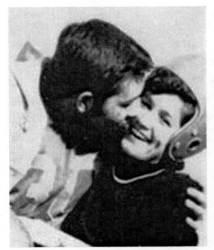 

Romelia Guardia Frisk

Academic:

San Felipe High School graduate, 1957. Selected 'Most Beautiful' by her graduating peers.

Nominated as 'Football Sweetheart' by the San Felipe Mustangs football team.

Professional Accomplishments:

After graduating from San Felipe, Romelia moved to California where she worked ten years with the Pacific Telephone Company. Later, during the time two of her youngest children were growing, she worked as an instructional aide for the local schools.

After that, she worked ten years full time with the Los Angeles County District Attorney's Office. This position involved communicating with the surrounding police agencies, the courts, and other social agencies.

Family:

Romelia's parents were Miguel and Antonia, who were both born in Del Río, Texas.

She had four siblings; Elida, Alfonso, Mickey, and Alda. Alfonso, who was the oldest, inspired Romelia, and the rest of us, to acknowledge the importance of a good education.

Romelia and her husband, Mike Frisk (Honorary 1957 classmate), have five grandchildren; Kelsey, Kaylon, Haley, Brylie, and Hannah. They spend their time coordinating necessary transportation, to and from, everywhere the kids need to go.

Perhaps coincidentally, the year after Romelia was crowned as 'Football Sweetheart,' her sister Alda, was also selected 'Football Sweetheart' during her graduating year.

Estela Salazar Spencer

Academic:
San Felipe High School graduate, 1957.

Professional Accomplishments:
After graduating from High School, Estela moved to Carlsbad, New Mexico in 1960.

Five years after she married, she moved to Clovis, New Mexico.

Estela has worked in hospitals and nursing homes all her married life. She has also worked for a home health agency, where she took care of the elderly, or disabled individuals. When she graduated from nursing school, Estela was awarded a Certificate of Perfect Attendance.

Estela retired from Clovis High Plains Hospital in 2006 after 20 years of service. She received 36 awards throughout that period. She plans to continue being involved in volunteer work.

Family:

Her parents were Alejandro and Julia, who are both now deceased. Estela was the oldest of eleven children:

Alejandro Salazar - (deceased), Oralia Salazar Hinojosa, Elvira Salazar (deceased), Gloria Salazar Hinojosa, Berta Salazar Zuniga, Guadalupe Salazar Ramos, Anita Salazar Molina, Santiago Salazar, Alfred Salazar (deceased), and Abelardo Salazar.

Estela had one daughter, Janie Coheen, who lives in Del Río, Texas.

Mario Barragan Jr.

Academic:
San Felipe High School graduate, 1973, the year of the consolidation of San Felipe and Del Río High School.

After graduation, Mario headed to San Marcos, Texas, to attend what was known then as Southwest Texas State University; now known as Texas State. He received a Bachelor of Arts degree with majors in Spanish and French during August of 1976.

Mario continued graduate studies and later received a Master of Arts degree from SWTSU in 1983.

Professional Accomplishments:
For a period of time, Mario returned to Del Río where he worked for the National Park Service.

Mario and his wife both taught for the San Marcos O.I.S.D. for most of their teaching careers until they moved to New Braunfels, Texas.

Mario taught several levels of high school Spanish and French in the San Marcos and the Comal School District.

Family:
Mario's parents were Mario Barragan Sr. and Elia, who were both born and raised in Del Río, Texas, where Mario Jr. would also someday be born. His mother Elia is deceased. Both of his parents had also

graduated from San Felipe High School. Additional family history is contained within Part I of this book.

Mario married a woman named Celia Siguero on November 12th 1977. He met her while studying at Southwest Texas State University.

Celia also received her Bachelor's and Master's degrees from SWTSU, majoring in Education during 1976 and 1977.

Celia taught Bilingual Education in several grade levels- 1st through 8th. She also taught in Specialized programs such as Title 1, English as a Second Language, Special Education, and Children with Dyslexia, in the San Marcos and Comal districts.

In 1996 and 1997, Mario and Celia spent their summers working with the Illinois Migrant Program in Princeville. They decided to retire together after thirty years. They have enjoyed traveling, volunteering, and being of service to those in need.

Mario and Celia have two children; Maricela and Mario Armando. They also have two grandchildren; Absedy and Sophia.

Their daughter, Maricela, earned a Bachelor of Arts degree in Business Administration from Southwest Texas State University. She also earned a certification in education.

Their son, Mario Armando, received a Bachelor of Arts degree in Business Administration from the University of Texas in San Antonio.

Oscar and Rosario Cardenas

Academic:

San Felipe High School graduates, 1958.

Oscar graduated with high honors, at the scholastic rank of Salutatorian. Impressively, his wife Rosario, also known as Chayo, was even placed above her husband's academic rank. She earned the distinction of graduating with highest honors as Valedictorian of her class.

Oscar received a Bachelor of Music Education degree in 1969, from Sul Ross University.

He went on to obtain a Master's degree in School Administration from Southwest Texas University in 1970.

Professional Accomplishments:

Oscar served as Superintendent Assistant for San Felipe Independent School District where he had the responsibility of Federal Programs, curriculum, personnel maintenance, and transportation.

He held a position with the U. S. Office of Education in Washington D.C. as a Senior Level Manager.

He received several awards for his contributions in the advancement of the Department of Health and Welfare.

Oscar also received a Distinguished Service award from the U. S. Commission of Education in Washington.

In 1982, Oscar served as the Bilingual Director for the Texas State Education Agency for twenty years.

Oscar and Chayo have formed The Advocacy Systems for Education, a consulting firm in Austin, Texas.

Family:

Oscar's parents were Felix Cardenas and Juana Moncada. He was born in the barrio of San Felipe. His father was born in Cuatro Cinegas Coahuila, Mexico, and his mother was born in Eagle Pass, Texas.

Oscar has five older siblings; Viola, Irma, Odelia, Graciela, and Felix Jr. One of the girls still lives in Del Río, Texas.

Oscar married Rosario Escamilla in December, 1963. As of the year of 2015, they have been married for forty-seven years. They have two sons; Oscar Adrian and Roberto Javier.

Oscar Adrian married a woman named Ana and gave Oscar three grandchildren; Adriana Mignon - 14, Oscar Alejandro - 10, and Adan Miguel - 7.

Joel Reyes

Academic:
San Felipe High School graduate, 1956. Selected 'Most Handsome' by his graduating peers.

For elementary school, Joel attended both; La Escuela Calaveras and La Escuela Amarilla.

Throughout high school, Joel was an avid and talented member of the San Felipe Marching Band.

After graduation he attended San José Junior College for two years.

Professional Accomplishments:
He was employed by the IBM Corporation in San José, California.

Family:
Joel was born in Del Rio, Texas. Both of his parents were also born in Texas. They lived their entire lives on 207 Frausto Street, which was two blocks from San Felipe High School.

Both of Joel's parents were strong advocates of the community and our beloved high school.

Joel's mother, Susana, became an advocate for many of Joel's friends. Because of her consistent and steadfast support for him, she also became a surrogate parent for several of us. She advised, counseled, and cared for Joel's circle of friends unconditionally, firmly, and without reservations. Sheced caring, understanding, and gentle towards all of us. Joel was fortunate to have had a mother that inspired his noble and caring ways. Susana was truly one in a million.

Joel had five siblings; Pedro Reyes Jr, Ramiro, Dolores, Bernice, and Susana.

Joel married a woman named Grace. Joel and Grace have 6 grandchildren who live in San José, California.

Joel and Grace spend a significant amount of their time providing transportation with a 'bus' van, a very appropriate vehicle, to shuttle their grandchildren to and from anywhere they need to go.

David Vela

Academic:

San Felipe High School graduate, 1957.

David attended *Our Lady of Guadalupe Catholic School* from 1st to 8th grade.

He was an active participant in the Spanish Club with Mr. Paz.

He was an assistant for Year Book and an advertisement manager with Mrs. Ware.

David attended Lewis Barber College in San Antonio, Texas. He also attended several training seminars to enhance his business.

Professional Accomplishments:

As his college experience indicates, David chose Barbering as his career.

David has proudly worked as a Barber for over fifty years. Sixteen of those years he worked at Laughlin Air Force Base Barber Shop.

The remainder his years as a Barber, he spent working in his own private business, well known as, *Vela's Barber Shop*.

Family: David

David's parents were; José G. Vela and Maia G, both of whom were born in Mexico. They came to the United States during the Mexican Revolution, just as most of our parents did. Later, they both became American Citizens.

David married a woman named Ofelia Moncivas. They have two children; David Vela Jr. and Dalinda Calvettie.

David and Ofelia have three grandchildren; Chris, Joseph, and Anthony Lee.

David's brother, Harvey G. Vela, also graduated from San Felipe High School, three years earlier, in 1954. Harvey later married Odelia Cardenas, who graduated from San Felipe the same year.

It's admirable that David has maintained such a thriving business and wonderful family for so many years. It is always a pleasure to see David continue activities and maintain contact with his graduating class.

I share his fond memories of swimming at 'La Presita' and his visits to Memo's Restaurant.

Frank Zuniga

Academic:

San Felipe High School graduate, 1957.

In 1953, Frank made a transition to San Felipe High School. In spite of the fact that he found the new environment challenging, he managed to adjust and move forward. Even though he had a late start in athletics, he managed to make all-district in football and track. He was also involved in baseball.

Most remarkably, in spite of many roadblocks after high school, with encouragement and support from his parents, he became the first person from the 'Rincon del Diablo' to receive a college degree.

Family:

Franks parents were Gabriel Moron Zuniga and Carolina. They were both immigrants from the state of Coahuila, in Mexico. They settled in Del Rio, Texas in the 1930's. His parents were both devout Catholics and firmly believed in education. They were determined that their children would receive a Catholic education. Frank and his three siblings all graduated from Our Lady of Guadalupe School.

Frank was born on December 9th, 1938 followed by brothers; Gabriel Jr, Ricardo, and Ernesto.

In 1950, the family experienced a tragedy, where it lost a son and brother, Gabriel Jr, as a result of an accident.

In 1966, Frank married a woman named Angelica Ramirez. They have four children:

Celia Zuniga Barrera, the oldest daughter, completed three degrees. She ultimately achieved a Doctorate in Education. She became, and as of 2015, is still the principal of Del Rio High School.

Alda Zuniga, the second oldest daughter, also obtained Bachelor and Master of Arts degrees. She is presently a counselor at Del Rio High School.

Sonia Zuniga, the third oldest daughter, earned Bachelor and Master of Arts degrees and is currently working on a business project in San Antonio, Texas.

Elsa Zuniga, the youngest daughter, completed a Bachelor of Science degree and is currently working for a corporation in the Boston area.

Frank encouraged his brothers Ricardo and Ernesto to further their education. As a result, they both persevered and received college degrees.

Ricardo completed a degree in education and Ernesto completed a degree in Engineering.

Ricardo passed away in 2012, while Ernesto retired and now lives in San Antonio, Texas.

Frank and Angelica's hope and devotion to education and their children, is beautifully evident and admirable.

Joe Gonzalez

Academic:

San Felipe High School graduate, 1957. Selected 'Most Likely to Succeed' by his graduating peers.

He attended grade school at La Escuela Calaveras where Mrs. Irene Cardwell was his first grade teacher. She was also his next door neighbor and Godmother.

In the fourth grade, Miss Calderon was Joe's teacher. His favorite memories of Miss Calderon was her excellent teaching and her use of an oak paddle with holes in it. This was her way of maintaining discipline. Joe remembers how effective her disciplinary system was.

Joe's favorite memory was during the Fifth grade when they had to wear a tie for dress-up on Fridays.

After he left the elementary years, he transferred to San Felipe Junior High, and then to San Felipe High School. He remembers his outstanding home room teacher, Miss Shirley Stiles, from Junior High

When Joe was promoted to the seventh and eighth grade he remembers, with utmost respect and admiration, the teachers he affirms were the best; Bobby Cuellar, Poncho Guardia, and Eddie Paredes.

High School were his best years. He was fortunate to have known some of the best teachers in High School such as; Mrs. Keller for Math, Mrs. Pasley for English, as well as several other outstanding teachers.

Joe was also very fortunate to have been surrounded by outstanding mentors and scholars such as; Arturo Cuellar and Tony Carvajal.

Immediately after graduation, he and several of his peers joined the Marine Corp. He was tested and scored extremely high- at the college level, achieving an I.Q. of 131. He was right up there with Arturo Cuellar and Tony Carvajal.

After he was discharged from the Military, he attended Sul Ross College for two years.

Professional Accomplishments:

After choosing to discontinue college, Joe quickly found an excellent job.

Family:

Joe married a woman named Fran, who is an honorary member of the class of '57. He considers himself 'Most Likely to Succeed' for having found her.

Joe's parents were Joe C. Gonzales and Josefa. He was the sixth child and third son, making him the baby of his family.

Dalinda (Dolly) Calderon

Academic:

San Felipe High School graduate, 1957. Selected 'Most Versatile' by her graduating peers.

Professional Accomplishments:

Dolly possesses an exemplary amount of administrative genius. Utilizing such a characteristic, she continues to be the central impetus for *Memo's* restaurant, a historical setting known by a significant number of people throughout the Southwest.

The glitter that Blondie Calderon and his brothers had ignited, lives on- simply because of the dedication and passion of our dear friend, Dolly. Her charismatic and relentless persona have been the necessary elements it takes to keep a business like *Memo's* shining throughout the years.

It is no wonder that she was named 'Most Versatile' by our graduating class. She is indeed most versatile and most precious.

Family:

Dolly's parents were Jose and Elida Martinez. Mr. and Mrs. Martinez were well known in the community and the schools. Mr. Martinez served as Principal of the San Felipe High School while his wife, Elida, maintained her social standing in various aspects of the school and community.

Dolly had one sister named Joelda. They both possessed prominent and enviable standings within the schools and community. They have served both areas with admirable distinction.

Joelda's significant leadership and conscientious involvement with the San Felipe Exes organization was held in high regard. I was particularly pleased to have had the opportunity to work with her during the time I was invited to serve as, Master of Ceremonies, for the Black and White Formal Ball in 2007. It was great to navigate those days with her outstanding and thoughtful guidance.

Carmen Sanchez

Academic:
San Felipe High School graduate, 1956.
After graduation, Carmen attended *San Antonio Commercial College* for one year, earning herself a business certificate.

Professional Accomplishments:
After earning her business certificate, Carmen worked as an office clerk typist at *Del Río Lumber*.
Her husband established his own plumbing business, developing an excellent network of business clients, while they lived in San Antonio.

Family:
Carmen married a man named Refugio Rodrigues. After their marriage, they moved to San José, California, where they stayed for ten years. They had two children while they were living in San José. Shortly

after having their daughter, Lydia in 1968, they moved back to Del Río in 1970, primarily to take care of Carmen's parents.

Carmen and her husband later moved to San Antonio, where by 2015, they had lived for 43 years.

Carmen's parents were Henry and Carmen, who both worked several jobs. Henry became a celebrated and gifted musician who was always available to perform in celebrations at weddings, dances, school proms, and other social events.

The highlight for this family, was the day that Carmen's mother completed her General Education Degree (GED) at the age of 75. The celebration of her graduation was, in itself, an honorable tribute to her tenacity for completing what had always been important to her and her family.

Carmen and Refugio have three granddaughters and one great granddaughter.

Carmen has one brother, Frank, and three sisters.

Frank graduated from San Felipe High School in 1950. He was married a woman named Mable Billings, who was also from the class of 1950. They had three sons and one daughter. He and Mable tragically lost their eldest son, Eddie Fran, at the young age of 20, due to a car accident.

Eddie's wife, Cecilia, was left a widow with a three month old daughter, Jennifer Piembert.

Frank's other children; Lee, who received a Bachelor of Arts degree in Industrial Arts, and Terry, who graduated from Del Río High School and attended the University of Texas, earning a Bachelor of Arts degree in Business.

One of Carmen's sisters, Socorro Sanchez, graduated from *San Antonio College* in 1953 and became a physical therapist at *San Rosa Hospital* and *Baptist Hospital*.

Another of Carmen's sisters, Grace, attended Beauty College in San Antonio, Texas, and completed a degree in Cosmetology. She also completed certification as an Emergency Medical Technician and worked for 18 years at Val Verde Hospital. She married Danny Chavira from the San Felipe graduating class of 1960.

Dr. Antonio Carvajal

Academic:

San Felipe High School graduate, 1957.

Completed Associate of Arts degree in San José, California.

Bachelors of Science degree in English and Speech from *Sul Ross State University*.

Master of Arts degree in Sociology and Special Education at *Texas A & M* in Commerce, Texas.

Doctorate in Education and Psychology from the *University of Northern Colorado*, in Greeley, Colorado.

My Post-doctoral education was completed at *Stanford University* and *Betty Ford Clinic* in Rancho Mirage, California.

Professional Accomplishments:

Completed forty-four years in Education; ten years in public schools and thirty-four years in Higher Education.

Family:

My parents were Ramon and Consuelo Carvajal. When I was born, they lived in Del Rio, Texas, where they lived their entire married life. My dad was also born in Del Rio, Texas, while my mother was born in Monterrey, Mexico.

My grandparents, Antonio and Francisca Ramirez, left Mexico during the Mexican Revolution. At that time, my mother, Consuelo, and her sister, Amparo, were about five years old. My grandparents settled in Del Rio, Texas, making their home in the barrio of "La Placita."

My parents had seven children; Ramon Jr, José (Prieto), Maruca (Maggie), Antonio (me), Francisco, Raul and Amparo (Payito). Two of my siblings, Ramon and José, are deceased.

My wife, Joanie, and I live in Greeley, Colorado. We have three children; Jennifer, Carmela, and Marc Anthony. We have three grandchildren; Taylor Maté, Alexander Kabacy, and Dustin Kim.

International and National Endeavors:

Professional consultant for the Peace Corp: Interventions for children with Autism in North Africa: Tunica, Gabes, Sfax, Jerba, and Timbactu.

Novascotia, Canada, Barcelona, Spain, Dublin, Ireland and Quito Ecuador, and the United States of America.

Recent Publications:

Essential Moments, Spring 2009
Embraced By Love (Abrazos de Carino) Fall 2013
The Roads We Traveled, Summer 2015

Honors:

American Association for Higher Education- Jaime Escalante Award: Stand and Deliver: Exemplary Programs in Higher Education for Youth at Risk. Chicago, Illinois.

Eliodoro Martinez

Academic:

San Felipe High School graduate, 1957.

When Eliodoro was of school age, he started elementary school at La Escuela Calaveras. When he graduated to the second grade, he attended *Our Lady of Guadalupe Catholic School*. He later attended La Escuela Amarilla. After he completed third through fifth grade, he transferred to San Felipe Junior High School.

After returning from his service in the Marine Corp, Eliodoro enrolled at *Sul Ross University*. Unfortunately, because of financial difficulties, he had to discontinue pursuing his higher education.

Professional Accomplishments:

Eliodoro and nine of his classmates joined the Marine Corp. Fernando Gonzalez joined the Navy. The friends that joined the service with Eliodoro were; Guadalupe Felan, Teno Flores, Ricardo Perez, Ruben Flores, Joe Linian, Joe Gonzalez and Alfonso Sanchez.

In November of 1960, Eliodoro was Honorably Discharged.

Five years after his marriage, Eliodoro started working for The National Life and Accident Insurance Company.

Family:

Eliodoro's parents were, Rosendo and Maria Alcala, both of whom had immigrated from Mexico in the early nineteenth century. They received their religious marriage ceremony at *Our Lady of Guadalupe Catholic Church*.

Eliodoro had seven siblings- four brothers and three sisters. The boys were named; Serapio, Luis, Resendo Jr, and Homero. The sisters were named; Aurora, Maria de Jesus, and Eloisa.

Serapio, Luis, and Maria de Jesus are deceased.

Eliodoro was the fifth addition to his family.

When Eliodoro was unable to find a job in California after his attempt at college, he returned to Del Rio. On July 15th of that year, he married a woman named Ricardita Perez.

Eliodoro and Ricardita have three children; Evelyn, John Edwards, and Jacqueline.

Evelyn earned a Bachelor of Science degree in legal service from *Kaplan University*. As of 2015, she is employed as a case manager in the Office of the Attorney General in Austin, Texas.

John Edwards earned an Associate of Arts degree from *Southwest Texas Junior College* and is employed as an account associate with *Cigna Insurance* in Austin, Texas.

Jacqueline graduated from the *University of Texas* and married a man named Jesse Macias. Together, they have four children- three boys and one girl. Jackie is employed by the *Methodist Hospital* as a senior accountant for financial services in Houston, Texas.

Eliodoro discontinued his insurance job after fifteen years. He later worked for the United States Postal Service for twenty four years, retiring in 2003.

Ricardita worked for the school district as a teacher's aide for 12 years. She retired in 1995.

Nelda Laing

Academic:
San Felipe High School graduate, 1957.
Tab Club, Pep Squad, Square Dance Club, English Club, DTUP Club, Radio Club, Coronet Club, FHA, and Newspaper Manager.

Dolores Treviño

Academic:

San Felipe High School graduate, 1957.

Band, Band Secretary, Band Treasurer, Radio Club, Tab Club, Leather Craft Club, Business Club Vice President. FHA, Dramatic Club 'Band Sweetheart'.

Teno Flores

Academic:
San Felipe High School graduate, 1957.
Football, Track, Baseball, Tab Club, Leather Crafting Club, Radio Club, Dramatics Club, Square Dance Club.

Ricardo Perez

Academic:

San Felipe High School graduate, 1957. Selected 'Most Popular' by his graduating peers.

Football, Baseball, and Basketball Captain, All-District Basketball, Guard Track Captain, Yearbook Photo Editor, Square Dance Club, Radio Club, Favorite Candidate, Tab Club

José Leonel Li'nian

Academic:
San Felipe High School graduate, 1957.
Band, Radio Club, Yearbook Assistant Art Editor, Football, Newspaper, Square Dance Club, Tab Club, Track, Dance Club

He has been a key factor in the preparation and meticulous planning of Class reunions from the beginning. We continue to be grateful for his dedication to the class of 1957.

After High School, Joe joined the Marine Corp along with Eliodoro, Joe Gonzales, and several other classmates.

Joe received a Bachelor's degree in education and taught elementary students for 12 years.

He received a Master's degree in counselling. He has been a counsellor for 23 years.

Amelia (Molly) Cardenas

San Felipe High School graduate, 1957. Selected 'Best All Around' by her graduating peers.

FHA Treasurer, Tab Club, Square Dance Club, Newspaper, Dramatics Club, Band, Pep Squad, Year Book Photo Editor, Business Manager, Advisor to Business Staff, Science Club, Student Congress Representative, Business Club, Dancing Club, Math Club, Coronet Club, Football Sweetheart Candidate.

Molly is currently involved in business endeavors. She has three children and is married to Jim Opperman. As of 2015, she lives in Indiana.

HONOR STUDENTS OF SAN FELIPE HIGH

YEAR	VALEDICTORIAN	SALUTATORIAN
1932	Antonio Morales	Ubil Frausto
1933	Balgumero Gonzalez	Clotilde Rangel
1934	Berta Morales	Oscar Cardenas
1935	Raul Valdez	Abdenago Rivas
1936	Josefa Portillo	Gilberto Salas
1937	Ildelfonso Dominguez	Aurelia Oroszco
1938	Xavier Viesca	Petra Soto
1939	Jane Morales	Frank Villarreal
1940	Irma Esqueda	Jesus Marquez
1941	Miguel Cantu	Olivia Sanchez
1942	Pedro Lomas	Refugio Ramos
1943	Raul Dominguez	Clemencia Burts
1944	Anna Jones	Tomas Contreras
1945	Aurelio Diaz	Elida Contreras
1946	Fermin Calderon	Frank Rubio
1947	Roberto Cuellar	Uriel Treviño
1948	Nephtali Gutierrez	Yolanda Hernandez
1949	Antonio Herrera	Carlos Diaz
1950	Teresita Rodriguez Raul A. Treviño	Alfredo Gutierrez
1951	José Luis Nanez	Carlos Barrera
1952	Fortino Guzman	Rosalinda Padilla
1953	Esther Gonzalez	Berta Irene Rodriguez
1954	Teresa Acosta	Guadalupe Arriaga
1955	Rosalinda Lara	Frenchie Rodriguez
1956	Enrique Barrera	Estela Espinosa
1957	Adrianna Maldonado	Joe Gonzales
1958	Rosario Escamilla	Oscar Cardenas

In Memoriam

57 years Later

Abigail Zapata   Henry Davis
Raquel Zapata   Olga Rodriguez
Jesus Chavira   Diamantina Perales
Manuel Cardenas   Alfonso Sanchez
Fernando Gonzalez   Gus Cardenas
Ruben Flores   Adolfo Moya

PART FOUR

Significant Truths and Revelations

CHAPTER THIRTY-FOUR

Essential Memories
(Recuerdos Esenciales)

We must remember how we finally arrived where we are. The turning points in our lives are often slow and inadvertent. Many times those turns are also calculated and thoughtfully planned. This is the way that a handful of leaders gathered on September 7th, 1929, to form the San Felipe Independent School.

There was merely a handful of leaders that named themselves the San Felipe Leadership Team. There were no formal elections that constituted this illustrious group. No one had to buy votes to become a member. There were zero bylaws and zero dues to pay. Only commitment was required.

Originally, there were two groups that took it upon themselves to lead the dream; the Plaza Brown Committee and the Leadership Committee. The two committees were apparently disguised as one. It was essentially one and the same, with the same tenacious group of folks. They were comprised of men and women, who arrived from various parts of Spain, Mexico, and other Latino countries- seeking refuge, freedom, new dreams, and acceptance in a new land.

These forefathers and foremothers arrived on boats, cargo trains, canoes, and some simply crossed the border by foot. As they arrived on the shores and borders of the United States of America, each family migrated to various parts of country. They typically migrated to places where they could find similar languages, ethnicities, customs, and lifestyles.

A very outstanding document, *A History of San Felipe*, was compiled and written by A. E. Gutierrez. It was mentioned and discussed in the Prologue section of this book by author Dave Gutierrez. He finely details the ways our group was initially separated from a broader community. The city of Del Río- a border town across from Villa Acuna, Mexico.

Because of its fascinating history, the central purpose for writing *The Roads We Traveled* was personal. It evolved from my interest of wanting to know how my friends, who shared many continuous days, weeks, months, and years- almost a lifetime, were doing these days- seventy years after we met in elementary school at either; La Escuela Calaveras or La Escuela Amarilla.

The descriptive design of this book required a research structure. It was a simple questionnaire that was answered by the students who graduated from our San Felipe High School between 1954 and 1959- on average, fifty six years after they graduated from high school.

My approach to gather as much information from my friends as possible, was in the form of a personal letter, where I explained the reason I was writing to them. Circumstances of having seen them at intermittent times during the years, such as at class reunions or other social occasions, provided an enthusiastic level of support for the project.

Eighty five percent of the questionnaire recipients responded to three specific questions: 'Will you share with me how you are doing these days?,' 'How are your families, parents, and siblings?,' and 'What level of education did you complete after graduating from high school?' I also encouraged submission of any additional information they wished to share such as; spouses, occupations, mobility, etc.

When my fellow classmates responded to the questionnaire for *The Roads We Traveled*, their detailed and comprehensive responses were reminiscent of a memoir- each one responding with an average of eight pages, outlining the, most insightful, and personal journeys they had traveled. They included emotional, professional, and personal aspects. They wrote about their essential moments. I responded to every single response. Personal conversations over the phone took place in great numbers. The process took over a year.

Through their writings and other communications, it was clear that remembrances of our high school years were nurtured in a fairy tale world. Each day was predictable. Our teachers and administrators were geniuses at replicating a special place, commonly known to us, as the land of Camelot.

Because of the fact that our community leaders knew that the City of Del Río, across the bridge, did not accept us, they prepared an environment for us that would compensate for the harsh and cruel realities of segregation and prejudice. Clearly, the saving grace in our days, was knowing that we had a place where we were embraced with unconditional acceptance.

Each evening, while preparing the narratives for each of my classmates' responses, I also read and saw earlier copies of San Felipe High's annual year books, El Conquistador. I was impressed with the amazing efforts that were displayed by teachers, parents, and administrators, who were devoted to recognize each student. In a personal manner, they heralded the many scholarly, social, and athletic activities, of each student.

I was also particularly impressed to see the ostensible theatric backdrops and wardrobes that, parents and teachers alike, had prepared when presenting students who had achieved special awards or recognitions.

When I graduated in 1957, the approach had unfortunately changed to a more simplistic format. If the mode of heraldry had continued, and if I had received an award, I imagine that I would have been regally introduced as 'Prince Antonio, from the House of Carvajal.' I really would have liked that. The honor would have made me feel like a Knight from the House of Don Quijote or something like that. Today, knowing my unforgiving and sarcastic friends, I would likely be remembered as Sancho Panza- the guy on the donkey.

When I responded to the influx of letters, sometimes with tears of gratitude, I too, rewrote traces of my essential memories. I was compelled to remember and share how our problems and needs within our own families were addressed during those early days. When we faced the dire needs for groceries, Aurelio Diaz's grocery store credit was invaluable. Emergent medications for a severe colic and other ailments were attainable from Panchito Hernandez's drug store, only a few steps from our home- also on credit. Small loans from friends and neighbors to supplement grocery needs or pay utility bills were also common. Many were never repaid. That was our Camelot.

The responses also addressed the steadfast loving support and caring from their parents, siblings, and friends. A recurring theme of faith was central to their lives. My tendency has always been to choose to live in a fantasy world, looking for only the good in people, while ignoring the ugliness of discrimination that surrounds us. Unfortunately, my naïve outlook was shattered when my dear classmates shared their personal recollections of bigotry and prejudice that they experienced during those years.

Even though I had seen and heard negative racial insults at my work place from customers at the drive-in theater, because of my naïveté, I ignored it. A fitting proverb says, 'Fish don't know they live in water.'

With racial segregation having been declared as unconstitutional in 1954, we thought better days would surely follow. In actuality, social and political climate was slow to change. The segregated culture that had shaped Del Río for years, would take many years, if ever, to be completely eradicated.

During my junior high school years, I sadly recall the many brutal and humiliating racist insults my older brothers had experienced when they walked the streets of Del Río. I also recall the somberness and loneliness my brother, Ramon, suffered when he returned after serving for four years in the United States Air Force in 1953.

I tried every possible way to encourage Ramon to talk to me. One evening when he laid down in his usual, dark room, I made efforts to encourage him to have a snack. A slant of sunlight fell through the roof on to his face and I could see tears accumulating in his eyes. I asked him if he could take a walk with me by the river before dark. On the evenings that he agreed, we would walk slowly, in silence, towards the river bank. Later we would return home. Quietly and sadly, as a broken man, he would softly say goodnight.

One particular evening, Ramon agreed to take a walk with me. While we walked, he surprisingly made efforts to speak. Almost as if mumbling to himself, I was barely able to hear his words, "I spent four years in the military." I listened carefully as he continued, "Most of those years, I was rejected as a person and as a soldier by the Anglos." He spoke solemnly, "They thought they were superior to me. They used to call me 'wet back.' I was forced to handle these idiots by isolating myself and pretending that all was fine." He reveled his saving grace, "I knew I would soon be home."

Ramon's sad story was not over. "Hermanito (my little brother), you know what really hurts me more than those days?" he asked, pausing briefly. "I feel more rejection, even here in my own town," he said. He sounded depressed, "I thought that things would be better after I came home." Then he said, "Not true. I am not accepted." Even though it was dark, I could sense his tears, "The people across the bridge are real bastards. I am not allowed to enter any public place. I couldn't even get a haircut last week."

Ramon, sitting on his bunk while
he was fulfilling his service

After our heart-to-heart, Ramon and I became soul brothers. That was also the day when I became worried and scared. I was determined not to be part of the City of Del Río terrain. I was dreadfully worried, wondering how Ramon would be able to trust again. What would it take for him to recover from the vicious and humiliating abuses he had experienced? My heart broke into pieces for him.

Blatant examples of discrimination experienced by some of my friends, the ones who graduated with me, also evoked personal disillusionment and profound sadness. Incredible as it may seem, at this point in my life, I must have been able to recreate a world of make-believe to think that only good things happened to us.

As I wrote the final pages of my work, I asked myself, how important can it be to know the truth? Well, It's very important. The truth is unfortunate, but discrimination and prejudice continues in all corners of America. Some of it is silent and some of it is blaringly loud.

Fortunately, today in America, the Fourteenth Amendment has been upheld to defend our equality, bolstered by the Civil Rights Act of 1964 and subsequent legislation which defends the rights of all citizens. Today, there is a greater amount of fairness in the areas of; employment, housing, marriage equity, education, gay rights, and a broad spectrum of numerous personal rights, than there was 50 years ago.

On a personal level, we can find ways to heal. For me, the best way to heal is through forgiveness. I have forgiven those who have discriminated against me, my friends, and my family. I have asked God to do the same. My faith has healed me.

Of the classmates who responded to my questions, each one of them enhanced my appreciation for the healthy world my teachers and parents created for us. Now I know what Mom meant when she said, "Estudia y callate" ("Study and keep quiet"). Even though when she said it, it better translated to 'Do your homework and shut up.' This was Mom's tool to keep us on course and focus on what was important to move forward. All my teachers were basically saying the same thing in their own way.

Because of the past that we shared together, I have immense respect and admiration for the many positive, personal and professional, hopes and dreams, shared by my friends. It is definitely clear that our life travels have been fruitful. Our faith and love has been good for us.

One question that had remained unanswered to me encompassed the reasons why the administrative leaders from the City of Del Río, in early 1887, initially decided to designate our parents and grandparents to an isolated corner of Del Río, known as San Felipe. They too were segregated, apparently upon arrival.

More recently, interviews with past teachers and the scrutiny of literatures regarding this question, provided one reasonable and acceptable answer: The City of Del Río was facing financial problems. They did not have the necessary funds to provide additional facilities to accommodate or house the influx of immigrants. They could not afford appropriate educational facilities for the children. There was a new emergent need which challenged leaders of San Felipe to create their own solutions for the needs of children that were requiring formal schooling.

An additional, assumptive explanation, is more serious. The City of Del Río intentionally used the first reason of financial starvation, as an excuse to separate and segregate Mexican children from the Anglo community.

Only social conscience can untangle this conundrum. Whether it was for the sole purpose of separating us from them, due to financial constraints, a geographic dilemma, or a purposeful and intentional expression of racial discrimination, we will never know.

In my heart of hearts, both deeply and sincerely, regardless of any of the reasons, what I have left today, is an enormous sense of gratitude for the stoic challenge Mr. Santos Garza, Mr. Rudolfo Gutierrez, and the rest of their team embraced.

They designed a paradise- a cocoon, that could never be destroyed or replicated in any corner of America. The sentiments and allegiance to our education were rooted deep in the soul of the community and in all of us, never to be uprooted.

All I know for certain is that if God, in his infinite wisdom, had not guided me and all of us to discover our fate in this economically devastated, but glorious environment, I would not have written this book. Ultimately, when there is self-discipline, forgiveness, love, and faith, any sordid or painful memories of misfortune or maltreatment fade away.

Each time I that I attempted to find a way to close this last chapter of my writing, I have found a tremendous need to reach out to my Escuella Amarilla third grade friend, Arturo Cuellar- to pretend that we are still on top of our favorite tree. It was the tree we used to climb during recess where our dreams were born. This is what he said to me:

"We had a support structure unlike any in the world. The belief system of the San Felipe School District was created by our teachers, our parents, our friends, and our community. They inspired us to believe that we could dream and prepared us to make those dreams a reality," and, "As we face the tomorrows of our lives, we still have the memories of our days together, and every now and then, we burst into laughter for no apparent reason. Sometimes a tear rolls down our cheeks, but a smile lights our face. Our loved ones have come to understand and call these occurrences, San Felipe moments."

CHAPTER THIRTY-FIVE

Conclusion

An incredibly brilliant teacher, Mr. Mauro Paz, had once inspired us to learn the history of the Constitution of the United States of America, appreciate the efforts of our gallant and patriotic, former president, Abraham Lincoln, and to learn to appreciate and admire, the difficult roads he had to travel, to become President of our country. He had also required each of us to be mindful of the amendments that the original Constitution had to include to respond to the needs of a changing America.

Three years after I graduated from San Felipe, while I was in college at San José City College in California, I attended a class in American history. Our history teacher, Mr. Bender, brought Mr. Paz's teachings back to life again as he reviewed key aspects of the original Constitution and the various Amendments that we studied while in San Felipe.

Even though he was not as personable as Mr. Paz, I do remember some of Mr. Benders' lectures very well. He elaborated considerably on the way the Amendments to the Constitution responded to new challenges during different times. During the third week of my attendance in his class, his lectures had already captivated me and my classmates.

The first resounding lecture I recall, was explicit; "despite the amendments that were made, African-Americans continued to be treated differently than whites in many parts of the country." In fact, he stressed, "in 1896, several state legislatures enacted laws that led to legally mandated segregation of the races."

During a following lecture, I was extremely disappointed to hear Mr. Bender say that one single law, known as the 'Jim Crow Law' of 1930, specifically decreed that blacks and whites could not use the same public facilities, ride the same buses, or attend the same schools. The law also declared that "it is unlawful for a negro and white person to play together or in a company of each other in any game of cards or dice, dominoes or checkers." He vehemently continued, "To add insult to injury, the law also declared: Marriages are void when one party is a white person and the other is possessed of one-eighth or more; Negro, Japanese, or Chinese blood."

Mr. Bender obviously knew well, that several of us were late to class because our buses were late. During one particular morning lecture, he seized the difficult nature of our transportation to make another point. He addressed the class, "How many of you get to this campus by bus?" His firm tone of voice woke me up. Several students and I quickly raised our hand. Secretly, I was hoping that he was ready to present suggestions that would offer free bus tokens or give me ideas of how I could avoid my three mile bus ride to my afternoon job.

Unfortunately for me, Mr. Bender's question was evidently rhetorical. He continued, "How many of you would be frustrated if the bus driver asked you to get off the bus because of the color of your skin or the color of your eyes?" The entire class groaned and there was a murmur of whispers. The audacious question incited firm opinions among us. Mr. Bender went on, "You must know that in our land of the free, similar regulations still exist."

My curiosity was piqued. I was wondering where he was taking this lecture. We listened intently as he spoke, "However, there is always hope in America the beautiful. Once upon a time, in 1892, an African-American man named Homer Plessy adamantly refused to give up his seat to a white man on a train in New Orleans, even though he was required to do so, by Louisiana state law. For this action, he was arrested."

Mr. Bender explained, "Mr. Plessy, contended that the Louisiana law separating blacks from whites on trains violated the 'equal protection clause' of the Fourteenth Amendment of the United States Constitution. He decided to fight his arrest in court. By 1896, his case had made it all the way to the United States Supreme Court. The Supreme Court ended up ruling against Homer Plessy. He lost his case."

Bender's follow-up lecture was captivating, "Listen carefully," he said, "Because of the Supreme Courts' ruling in Plessy vs. Ferguson, which resulted in the defeat of the Homer Plessy's case and other similar cases, many people in America continued to support the concepts of the 'Jim Crow Law' and other laws that supported segregation."

During one particular lecture, Mr. Bender impressed upon us with a hint of sarcasm, "If you are ever interested in becoming a lawyer, you will learn how colleges in our 'America the beautiful' were blatantly rejecting black students for admission into law school during those days." Unrelentingly, he added, "However, listen to this…" He snapped his fingers, "Listen carefully!" He elaborated, "When the students filed discrimination charges in the courts, the courts ruled in their favor. That was indeed a great victory for legal rights."

As Professor Bender's class continued, he was always challenging us to look at him whenever the content of his lecture would be included in his weekly quiz. When he did, we listened. On one such occasion, he said, "Most recently, children who were black were not allowed to attend public schools with white students." He obviously understood the inconvenience and pain of his statement, due to the fact that, he was an Anglo with a black child himself. "Why?" he asked. He submitted his own answer, "To this day I don't know, but again, it seems that the color of their skin was evidently the capricious reason."

Mr. Bender commonly stood firm on his platform, holding himself up high. Once again, he spoke passionately, "Listen to this!" he demanded. He snapped his fingers again, "Listen carefully! One parent refused to accept the biased decision." He elaborated, "Mind you, only one parent was angry that a school in Topeka, Kansas, had the gall to deny his child and other black children, access to their white school, which was just a few blocks away." He explained that a man named Oliver Brown, the child's parent, filed a class action lawsuit against the school district. Brown claimed that the Topeka School District violated the Constitutions' 'Equal Protection Clause' that is part of the Fourteenth Amendment. Sadly, Mr. Brown lost his case.

Mr. Bender excitedly and proudly announced, "Mr. Brown was not a quitter. He appealed the case to the Supreme Court. The Supreme Court consolidated five other similar segregation court suits, which also included Mr. Homer Plessy's case. After many months of negative encounters and arguments in the courts, solutions became evident."

Professor Bender was delighted to share with us that our country had made a gigantic leap towards eradication of the segregation of children in the public schools in America. He was extremely pleased to announce to us that on May 17th, 1954, U.S. Chief Justice of the Supreme Court, was able to bring all justices to agree to support a unanimous decision, which declared segregation in public schools to be unconstitutional. The Chief Justice also required that the attorney generals of all states that had laws permitting segregation in their public schools, to create and submit plans of how they were to proceed with desegregation with 'all deliberate speed.'

Our inspiring and brilliant professor, Mr. Bender, read the findings of the court verbatim, eloquently, and with a flare of personal pride:

"Brown vs. Board of Education decreed that the segregation of children in the public schools was a violation of the 14th Amendment and was therefore unconstitutional. The historic decision marked the end of the 'separate but equal' precedent set by the Supreme Court nearly sixty years earlier, and served as a catalyst for expanding the civil rights movement during the decade of the 1950s. The most significant victory was the Civil Rights Act of 1964 that outlawed discrimination."

Most significantly, today, because of the tenacious efforts of Mr. Oliver Brown and his friends, the Fourteenth Amendment has become the central legal defense used by citizens when their personal freedoms had been violated.

Mr. Bender's plethora of lectures at San José City College, convinced me that Congress, in many years past, was insightful to know that laws to protect the freedoms defined in the Constitution would be imperative. Now citizens in America would benefit from the same personal freedoms we enjoyed in our San Felipe school.

From experience, I know that this important legislation did not eradicate racial injustice, but for the first time, Professor Bender made me realize how important it was to be on the way to Equal Rights.

Somebody did Something Wrong Somehow

Today, fifty five years later and after having spent forty-four years on teaching in public schools and higher education, I wanted to bring this manuscript to a meaningful and happy ending. I learned through reading published literature, that our school, the San Felipe Independent School District was consolidated with Del Río Independent School District in 1971.

Apparently such a consolidation was actually the result a fall out from an integration case that had developed in East Texas- a case which had nothing to do with Del Río schools originally. (Braudaway 2000)

Judge William Wayne Justice of the federal court in Eastern District of Texas began studying an integration case brought by the United States Department of Health, Education and Welfare (HEW) against the segregation of a number of "All Negro" school districts in East Texas in the fall of 1970. That was 16 years after the Fourteenth Amendment ruled that segregation was unconstitutional.

In the process, Judge Justice assumed jurisdictional authority over all Texas schools, including those in Del Río. Both HEW and the court suggested that consolidation of the minority districts with neighboring ones might be constitutionally required.

In Del Río, Justice ultimately decided that lesser remedies would prove insufficient to resolve all of the different issues brought to the courts by different government agencies. The judge abolished both Del Río's school districts and ordered them to consolidate into a single, city-wide district. The judge also ordered the city-wide district to adopt both districts' names so that the new districts' full name is currently San Felipe Del Río Consolidated Independent School District.

I know that I should have known that this change would occur. Because of my allegiance to my San Felipe High School, and the fact that the consolidation occurred, I was personally challenged to review other litigation that pertained to segregation of Mexican American children in Texas Public Schools that were in violation of the Fourteenth Amendment.

I had to go back to my graduate days at Texas A&M in Commerce City, Texas, to refresh academic concepts I learned as a graduate student in Education and Sociology. At that time the terms Culturally Deprived,

Culturally Disadvantage, Linguistically Variant, and Children with "Deficit Thinking" were common terms reflected in the literature.

My search was easier than I thought. One of the highlights of my research guided me to an outstanding manuscript published by Dr. Joel Vela, Professor of History. In his manuscript he traces the legal history of the various court cases that addressed the practice of segregation of Mexican American children in the public schools from 1930 to 1970 (Vela 2012).

In each of these cases the defense teams, those in support of segregation, consistently made reference to the same cultural deficit model professionals in the field of Sociology and Education commonly cited in the field (Carter 1970).

These are precisely the terms public schools used to justify placement of minority children away from the educational mainstream. Labels of "Cultural Deprivation and Cultural Disadvantage", "Language Delayed", were used to justify placing minority children in segregated public school buildings away from children in the regular classroom.

During the early years of the 70's, public education that included the field of Special Education, also participated in the practice of labelling a child who came from poverty. The term Familial Mental Retardation was used to describe the nature of mental deficiency caused by social-cultural or cultural-familial factors.

The term was a perfect waste basket category for public schools to label and place Mexican American children in Special Education classes who scored one standard deviation below the Mean Score on an Individual Standard Test of Intelligence (Mercer 1970).

During my first nine years of teaching Special Education in the public schools, administrators used the term 'Six Hour Retarded.' Even though these children functioned within the normal limits of their cultural groups before and after school, they were labelled mentally handicapped during their school day. Ironically, these children were only retarded during the six hours they were in school (Dunn 1968).

It's important to note that currently, personnel from the U.S. Department of Education is rigorously monitoring the disproportion of Racial and Ethnic Groups in Special Education.

There have been many court cases that addressed the topic of segregation of Mexican American children in the public schools. After reviewing some of these court cases, it became sadly clear to me that the arbitrary and calculating tendencies to remove minority children from the mainstream of the public schools continues.

For personal reasons, perhaps because of pride I have maintained through the years of living in poverty, I was compelled to review a 1945 segregation class action lawsuit filed by Gonzalo and Felicitas Mendez, and other parents, in Westminster School District in Orange County, California, which was blatantly repulsive.

The reason the defense attorneys used to separate their Mexican American children from the regular classroom was because "they were unfit and incapable to attend an "Anglo School". The defense argued : "Mexican Children possess contagious diseases, have poor moral habits, were inferior in their personal hygiene, spoke only Spanish and lacked English speaking skills".

It is unfortunate that American public schools must continue to be monitored to prevent irresponsible and blatant disregard, as well as disrespect for the legal and personal rights of families and their children.

It is no wonder that a study conducted by John Hopkins released in 2007, 185 Texas High Schools were labelled 'drop out' factories (Sharrer and Caputo, 2011).

It is important to add that in my follow-up review of the status of the 'Drop-out' factory syndrome, after the term went viral, schools seem to be addressing the problem more seriously by incorporating multiple community efforts. (Watts, 2011).

Also, in my opinion, it seems imperative that local school boards continue to review statistical information gathered by the National Center for Education Statistics and periodically analyze the condition and progress on school retention in their districts.

EPILOGUE

Saved By The Bell

When the bell rang at the school across the bridge, we never heard it. Therefore we didn't answer. We had our own school and our own bell to answer.

We must remind ourselves, that it was not a congressional decision, or the Office of Education that determined the needs of our community. It was simply a handful of intelligent and proud community leaders that designed an immensely creative paradigm that my classmates and I still remember today as Camelot.

Our Camelot evolved from the heart of the community. It was nourished by the parents and the excellence of superior and devoted teachers, both Hispanic and Anglo, who inspired us with caring, rigor, discipline, challenge, and honesty. This concept can and should be, replicated again, somehow.

Our parents, supported by our teachers and administrators knew nothing about the Deficit Model in Sociology that cautions us about the impact of poverty, or the disadvantage of language variations between home and school. It is true that a significant number of us were raised in economically disadvantaged homes. Most of the types of jobs our parents had, because of their limited education, were at entry levels.

In spite of our heritage, our respectful teachers and administrators did not discriminate us. Instead of experiencing isolation, our teachers encouraged participation. Instead of perceiving ourselves as linguistically impaired, we perceived ourselves as linguistically gifted. We learned and spoke two languages fluently. Instead of seeing ourselves as culturally deprived we viewed ourselves as culturally enriched. Instead of feeling neglected, we felt protected.

Most significantly, instead of our teachers making us feel doubtful and inferior, they knew ways to make us feel superior. They constantly enhanced the powerful hopes young people were eagerly grasping for, with the hope of becoming a valued person.

Valued persons we did become. Over ninety percent of the students, that attended San Felipe High School, graduated with a high school diploma. Some students left school to get jobs to help their family. We didn't have any 'push outs' or 'flunk outs.' Those who left, left by choice.

During the past two years, while I was writing this book, I was able to identify the number of high school Individuals that graduated from San Felipe High School from 1948 to 2008. Each class included at least 32 individuals. Fortunately, I was also able to track the numbers of individuals that graduated with scholarly honors during each of those years. Those names and years are listed in Part Four of this book.

The graduates from San Felipe represent every level of profession from; physicians, attorneys, public and private school teachers, college professors, business persons, writers, artists, engineers, nurses, social workers, service providers, and both public and private sectors.

It's important to share that a number of the individuals that chose teaching as a profession, returned to San Felipe High School to become teachers; Mr. Paz, Mr. Diaz, Mr. Ramon, and Mr. Paredes as well as several of my graduating peers.

San Felipe is a legacy that doesn't end. Anywhere we are, the years that we knew each other live one as brilliant memories of our days together. I even miss the years that my family's poverty was at its worst. Even the bad days were good.

Another significant recurring theme reflected in the narratives that were returned to me through questionnaires, were messages of affirmations about personal warriors that were there to stand by us through difficult times. Among these were parents, brothers and sisters, friends, relatives, neighbors, community advocates. and teachers. Because of them, it's apparent that love, resiliency, and self-discipline continue to guide the lives of our children, and their children.

Children must be been inspired to believe in themselves and follow their personal stair ways to success. Success is contagious, and indeed, familial. Years later, when they are grown, they too, will realize that they were valued. That's how America will continue to change for the best.

For us, the graduates of San Felipe, we have faced the tomorrows of our lives. We acknowledge that King Arthurs' Knights of the Round Table have vanished. The land we knew as Camelot is gone. We do know, however, that because we were given a temporary armor that prepared us for the tough years of today, most of us have been able to reach back, finding strength in what we have left behind.

BIBLIOGRAPHY

Braudaway, D. "Desegragation in Del Rio, Journal of South Texas, Volume 13, Number 2, Fall 2000, pages 24-265.

Braudaway, D. "Old San Felipe High School". Southwest Texas Jr. College. 1999.

Carter, T. P. (1970). Mexican Americans in School: A History of Educational Neglect. New York: College Entrance Examination Board.

Dunn, L. (1968) Special education for the mildly Retarded. Is much of it justifiable? Exceptional Children, 5-24.

Gutierrez, D. (2014). Patriots from the barrio. Xlibris Publications.

Mercer, J. (1972). Sociological Factors in the Educational Evaluation of Black & Chicano Children. Presented at the Tenth Annual Conference on Human and Civil Rights of Educators and Students. National Education Association. February 20, 1972.

Posney, Alexa. (2007, April 24). Disproportionality of racial and ethnic groups in special education. United States Department of Education. Office of Special Education and Rehabilitation Services.

Regua, Nannete. (2007, October 3). Mendez v. Westminister Case. Retrieved from www.Mendexs v. Westminsterncase.com.

Sharrer & Caputo. (2011). IDRA International development research association. John Hopkins University.

Vega, J. E. (2012) The education of the Mexican American: The New Emerging Underclass. International Journal of Humanities and Social Science. Volume 2 No. 14.

Watts, Lisa. (2011, February. Number of "drop factories declines. Jonh Hopkins Magazine.

END NOTES

1. General History of the Community of San Felipe, Del Rio, Texas. Antonio Gutierrez.
2. Integration Case Could Be Landmark. Del Rio News –Herald, April 14, 1971, page 13. "By compelling state education officials to exercise power to desegregate schools for (minorities), a statewide suit would conserve time and legal resources which would otherwise be expended on district- by - district suits". Rangel and Alcala, "Project Report." Page 375.
3. Angelitos Negros: (http://en.wikipedia.org/wiki/Angelitos_negros)
4. The History of Jim Crow (http://www.jimcrowhistory.org/history.htm). Ronald L. F. Davies
5. Teaching with Documents Related to Brown v. Board of Education (http://.www.archives.gov/education/lessons/brown-v-board/)
6. History of Brown v. Board of Education (http://www.uscourts.gov/educational_resources/get involved/federal courts_activities/brown-...)
7. The United States Bill of Rights: First 10 Amendments to the Constitution. (https://www.aclu.org/united_states_bill_rights)
8. National Center for Education Statistics (NCES). (http://en.wikipedia.org/wiki/National_Center_for_Education_Statistics)
9. The Constitution (http://www.lesisnexis.com/constitution/amendments_howitsdone.asp)
10. Primary Documents in American History (http://loc.gov/rr/program/bib/ourdocs/14thamendment.html)

11. The Supreme Court-Separate is Not Equal. (http://americanhistory.si.edu/brown/history/1-segregated/supreme-court.html)
12. Abraham Lincoln —Biography-Civil Rights Activist, Lawyer, U.S. Representative, U.S,... (http://www.bioraphy.com/people/abraham-lincoln-9382540)
13. United States Declaration of Independence (en.wikipedia.org/wiki/United_States_Declaration_of_Independence)
14. Oratorical Year Book for 1865: Being a collection of The Best Contemporary Speeches Delivered in Parliament, at the Bar, and on the Platform. (https://archive.org/bookreader/ie7/print.php?id=brahamlincoln00emer&se...)
15. Spark Notes: Wordsworth's Poetry: Ode: Intimations of Immortality (http://www.sparknotes.com/poetry/wordsworth/section3.rhtml)
16. Brown v. Board of Education-Wikipedia, the free encyclopedia (http://en.wikipedia.org/wiki/Brown_v._Board_of_Education)
17. Jim Crow Laws-Wikipedia, the free encyclopedia (http://en.wikipedia.org/wiki/Jim_Crow_laws)
18. Our Documents-13th Amendment to the U.S. Cohstitution: Abolition of Slavery (1865) (http://www.our.docements.gov/gov/doc.php?flash=true&doc=40)
19. School Desegregation and Equal Educational Opportunity (http://www.civilrights.org/resources/civilrights101/desegregation.html)
20. History of Brown v. Board of Education (http://www.uscourts.gov/eductional-resources/get-involved/federa-court-activities/brown)
21. Santos-Garza-Father of San Felipe School (http://vvchc.net/marker/Garza%20narrative.html)
22. 14th Amendment to the U.S. Constitution: Primary Documents of American History (http://www.lo.gov/rr/program/bib/ourdocs/14thamendment.html

CPSIA information can be obtained at www.ICGtesting.com
Printed in the USA
LVOW11s0352280515

440129LV00001B/1/P